A Strategy For Life

By Marion Cooper

Copyright © 2018 Marion Cooper

All rights reserved. No part of this publication may be reproduced, stored in a retrieved system or transmitted in any form or by means, electronic. Mechanical, photocopying or otherwise, without the prior written consent of the publisher. Short extracts may be used for review purposes.

Unless indicated, scripture quotations are taken from The Holy Bible, New International Version®, NIV®, Copyright ©1973, 1978, 1984, 2011 by Biblica, Inc.®

Used by permission. All rights reserved worldwide.

ISBN-10: 172341770X
ISBN-13: 978-1723417702

Deep Blue Publishing
c/o Revive Church
Bridlington Avenue
Kingston upon Hull
HU2 0DU, ENGLAND

DEDICATION

For my children, Jason, Jarrod, Victoria & Zachary.

Thank you for all the joy, laughter and love you have bought into my life.
Truly you are my 'heritage' and 'reward'. Psalm 127:3

CONTENTS

PREFACE ... 1

SECTION 1: A Strategy For Life

1. A Strategy For Life ... 4
2. "Be Strong" ... 7
3. Debt ... 10
4. Glorify God In Your Body ... 14
5. Choices ... 17
6. People ... 21
7. Surviving The Credit Crunch ... 24
8. Success ... 27

SECTION 2: Dealing With Rubbish In Our Lives

9. When It's Alright To Be Angry Part 1 ... 31
10. When It's Alright To Be Angry Part 2 ... 34

11	We Are Not Ignorant Of His Devices	37
12	Spring: Clear The Clutter	40
13	Who Am I?	47
14	Compromise	50
15	Are We Becoming A Marginalised Majority?	53

SECTION 3: Family

16	Children	57
17	Worth Fighting For Part 1	61
18	Worth Fighting For Part 2	65
19	Marriage: The "F" Plan	69
20	Attitudes To Sex Part 1: To Wait Is Best	73
21	Attitudes To Sex Part 2: Bible Blessed Sex	76
22	Christmas Memories	79
23	Keep Christ In Christmas	82
24	We Are A Grandmother	85

SECTION 4: Spiritual Keys

25	Time	89
26	Power In Worship	93
27	Calling	96
28	Suffering For Jesus	100
29	Prayer Principles	103

SECTION 5: The Mature Years

30	How Old Is Old?	107
31	"I Know That My Redeemer Lives"	110
32	Journey's End	113

SECTION 6: When Storms Rage

33	It Is Alright Part 1	117
34	It Is Alright Part 2	120
35	It Is Alright Part 3	123
36	Hope Does Not Disappoint	126

SECTION 7: Submission

37	Submission	130
38	Submission In Marriage	135

SECTION 8: We Are A Chosen People

39	We Are A Chosen People	139
40	Maintaining Passion	143

SECTION 9: Forgiveness

41	Forgiveness Part 1	147
42	Forgiveness Part 2	150
43	Forgiveness Part 3	153

SECTION 10: Being An Influence

44	My City, Kingston-Upon-Hull	157

45	"Do Not Oppress Foreigners In Any Way"	161
46	Ambassador For Christ	165
47	Joy	168
48	Our Core Values	172
49	Speak Up	176

SECTION 11: Changes

50	The Why And How Of Transition	180
51	Leaving With Our Blessing: Our Natural Children	186
52	Leaving With Our Blessing: Our Spiritual Children	189
	EPILOGUE	192
	ABOUT THE AUTHOR	194

PREFACE

This book is based on a series of, mostly unconnected, articles written for Assemblies of God national monthly magazine "Joy" around the year 2000. I was limited to one thousand words and the magazine produced them initially, as aimed at women, although they weren't originally written as such and eventually just became a regular column.

One reader commented that they were basically good, down-to-earth common sense. I like that because that's who I am. I also hope you see humour, empathy and sincerity.

I also hope wisdom is evident because it seems to me that godly wisdom is the single most important key to living a successful Christian life.

I have called this book, "A strategy for Life", because as I look at God's word, that is what I am seeking, the key to living for Jesus today. How can I be a woman of God in today's society? How can I succeed as a wife, as a mother, in my career and ministry? How can I touch my generation, my world for God now?

A secondary title would be, "An Opinionated Woman", because that also, is who I am! I just recently heard a preacher say, "Too many of us have opinions and this is wrong". He then went on for an hour to give us his opinion!

I love this young man of God and know what he was trying to say, basically that there are, in the church, "too many chiefs and not enough Indians", which of course is wrong, we must honour leadership. But in my opinion, we should all have an opinion!

This world is full of people who, whatever happens in their environment, do not seem to care, have no opinion, and remain silent. Their mantra could be, "Whatever."

The times in which we live, need people who will stand up and say "This is wrong, this is not godly." Or, conversely, to applaud righteousness and godliness whenever it occurs.

It is right to hold strong opinions, as long as I realise that mine is not the only opinion, nor is it the most important. And should my opinion on anything differ from the word of God, it is my duty to bring it sharply into line with God's, as I understand it.

I urge you, have an opinion. Care about the world in which we live, speak out for this and future generations. The enemy wants us to believe it is futile, that our opinions and our voice will be lost in the wind, that the tide cannot be turned or even that the subject of our concern is unimportant and trivial, but he would, wouldn't he?

If your opinion should differ from mine, that too is brilliant, at least we've been encouraged to think about what we believe.

SECTION 1

A Strategy For Life

Chapter One
A Strategy For Life

When I first became a Christian, some 47 years ago, I was given a little booklet emphasising the importance of 2 Timothy 2.15, "Be diligent to present yourself approved to God, a worker who does not need to be ashamed, rightly dividing the word of truth."

I don't know if I totally understood its meaning then or if I fully do today! But the message it placed in my heart has remained with me all these years and is the theme of almost all my ministry and certainly my life values: The Bible holds the secret of a strategy for life and if we seek to live by it, by His help, we will live successful lives, well pleasing to Him.

In the years that followed my conversion and certainly while we have been in church leadership, I have been deeply distressed by the number of Christians leading damaged and defeated lives in at least certain areas. During ministry, counselling or just generally talking, it has become clear that what many are seeking isn't necessarily a modern phenomenon, because it was also the request of Naaman to Elisha, "Call upon your God, wave your hand over me and heal my leprosy." 2 Kings 5:11. And I certainly understand that desire, I too would like instantaneous answers to my problems! "Lord wave your magic wand and change my spouse, my child, my bank account, my health, my addictions, my bad habits, change my life, now!"

Sometimes by His grace, God does just that, but much more often, my experience has been that God is there to help, direct, guide and encourage. His plan is that we have "a strategy for life" and work out our own problems until we come to a place of victory in that area. The book of Proverbs sings the virtues of wisdom for life. Do this and you will succeed, do that and you will fail. James 1:5 tells us that if we lack wisdom, we should ask God for it and He, without recriminations, will give it to us. Wisdom in our finances, wisdom in our marriages, wisdom to raise our children, wisdom in our ministries, wisdom in our jobs, wisdom in our relationships, wisdom to stay fit and well.

Let me give you an example. If I was deeply in debt, I am pretty certain that my desire would be that God would come and turn my red bank balance black immediately! And certainly, I would be praying and seeking God about this need. But Godly wisdom says I should look at why I am in debt. Am I unwise in my spending, do I have a budget? Where could I economise? Am I honouring God and tithing? Have I caught this world's materialism and credit culture? A more mature prayer would be, "God help me to get out of this mess and give me wisdom with my finances." If God did come with immediate answers, there is a really strong probability, that without altering our behaviour, we would soon be back in exactly the same position as before.

God gives us wisdom so that we can retrain ourselves in that area, so we become overcoming and victorious and not defeated. He gives us that strategy for life, the vast majority of which can be found in His Word.

Let me just counter this by saying, when we know there is absolutely nothing more we can do, that we are living wise, obedient lives, that's when He will come in and miraculously change the situation. In our years in Gibraltar, living as missionaries on a very meagre pay and raising two children, being extremely economical with our money, we at times knew totally miraculous financial provision. During one period, each month a bundle of banknotes was pushed into our post box, no envelope, no note, nothing, just miraculous provision.

When we become Christians, we are told to "walk in the spirit", but that doesn't require that we remove our brains! God's plan for us is that we become mature and perfect, lacking nothing. God's plan for us, His people, is that we have life skills, that we have wisdom, that in our everyday ordinary lives, we glorify Him. God's plan for us is that by His wisdom, we are role models to the world, that they seek our advice.

When I look into God's word, I am not really too interested in the meaning of the third toe on the foot of the statue in Nebuchadnezzar's dream! My husband loves those types of studies and I can see they are interesting, but when I look into God's word, I want to know how I can live a victorious, joyful, overcoming life for Jesus today. How can I avoid depression or unforgiveness? How can I raise my teenage son? How can I keep my marriage happy and passionate? How can I walk closer to Jesus? How can I be a testimony today?

"Every part of scripture is God-breathed and useful one way or another - showing us truth, exposing our rebellion, correcting our mistakes, training us to live God's way. Through the word, we are put together and shaped up for the tasks God has for us." 2 Timothy 3:16 The Message.

Chapter 2
"Be Strong"

In the Bible, we are often exhorted to "Be strong". In the Old Testament, God commands Joshua as he undertakes a huge task to "Be strong" (Joshua 1:6). Then again in the New Testament, Paul encourages the church in Ephesus to "Be strong" in spiritual battle (Ephesians 6:10).

First of all, let's look at what it means to "be strong". It is not to be arrogant, bossy, loud or over opinionated. The dictionary says to be strong is: Strong physically, mentally, morally (and spiritually), powerful, effective, decided and most importantly, difficult to capture! And if you notice, it is a command, "Be strong". And that's a bit scary; because the truth is even the most mature of us don't always feel strong. But that is what I love about God, He gives us a command and then He gives us His Spirit to help us to fulfil it, "My grace is sufficient for you, for My Strength is made perfect in weakness" 2 Corinthians 12:9.

"Lord you command me to be strong, take my weakness and exchange it for your strength."

I had been meditating on these scriptures, their meaning, the fruit of obeying, when I was called on to minister (pray for) during a couple of conferences we had at our church. On at least two occasions, I was praying for beautiful women in obvious pain and distress, not physically but emotionally and spiritually. Although I was not meant to be counselling at all, (we were in a prayer line,) these women began to tearfully speak of their pain, rejection, depression and fears, one even referring to rejection in the womb. On each occasion, I continued to pray and minister, feeling a huge compassion for these Christian women who knew the sacrifice of Jesus, who were saved and yet bound. They were not free. This compassion for my sisters was quickly turned to anger at the enemy who can so lie and deceive us; he robs us of our freedom, our joy, our peace and our life. Why do we let him do it to us? Why do we lay down under his lies? How can he hoodwink us so easily? How can he make us, God's children, so weak and unhappy?

"Be aware of the devil's schemes," the Bible says, 2 Corinthians 2:11.

Be wary of counselling, be wary of a mind set that says "poor me, how badly I have been treated."

I, as much as anyone, and perhaps more than some, struggle with self-pity. But I have learned that to sit and dwell on my pain, hurt and rejection is unproductive and negative and turns me into what I do not want to be, a weak woman whom Satan has bound. James 4:7 says, "Submit to God, resist the devil and he will flee from you."

a) "Submit to God" by declaring His creative word over your life. "I am accepted." "I am forgiven." "I am chosen." "I am strong." Speak it out loud so the enemy can hear!

b) Submit to God by seeking to bring your life into line with God's word, repent if the Holy Spirit convicts of any sin - e.g. unforgiveness.

c) Resist the devil! How is it that we know exactly how to get cross with our spouse and certainly know how to raise our voice with our children, (Yes we do, tell the truth now!), but when it comes to resisting the devil, our assertiveness flies out of the window! The Bible says, "Resist the devil and he has to flee from you." James 4:7. Command him to go, declare he has no part in your life. Let's be American "Kick his butt!" Or let's be scriptural and "Trample him under your feet!" Don't be polite and English, you can get angry, determined and aggressive, it is allowed!

d) Then fill your life and heart with positive food from God and His word. Speak to your soul as King David did, "why are you cast down O my soul, hope in God." Psalm 42:5. Count your blessings.

A quote from my husband, "What you feed grows, what you starve dies."

Feed your heart self-pity, it will grow. Feed your heart on the affirmation of God's word and that will grow. Starve your heart of negative thoughts, they will die.

On a very practical level, look after yourself. Eat healthily, get enough sleep, take care of your appearance. See also if there is a trigger to depression, anxiety, etc. and avoid it. I personally know, I have to get out of the house for a period each day; I hate being in the house all the time. I am also made low by too heavy a schedule, some people thrive on this, I don't, so I avoid filling every day too heavily.

God has plans for you and me, plans to prosper us, to give us a hope and a future. We mustn't allow the enemy to rob us of all God has for us. Let us be strong and not easily captured.

"For God has not given us a spirit of fear (or depression, anxiety or weakness) but of love, power and a sound mind." 2 Timothy 1:7

Chapter 3
Debt

A few months ago, I was in the bank making some transactions. At the till next to me a very shabbily dressed young woman was being served. To my annoyance, the middle-aged female cashier was trying to persuade her into a credit card. Back and fore the discussion went, the young woman bravely trying to say she didn't want a credit card, she had just paid off her debts and didn't trust herself with another card. The smartly dressed cashier asked did she know she needed a credit card to book hotels! The struggling young woman looked as if she barely had the bus fare home, the whole conversation was incongruous.

After the young woman had left, thankfully without a credit card and I had finished my transactions, I moved over to the other till and told the cashier calmly and politely "I realise that you have targets to meet, but I just feel that what you just did was incredibly unethical." Out of control debt is the scourge of our generation. While I realise that many of our jobs put pressure on us to put pressure on others, God gives us wisdom to be honourable.

While this article was written at a time of particularly easy credit, which eventually helped contribute to the international credit crisis, the principles within hold true today.

We were at our local supermarket the other week and as I waited for my husband David to collect a trolley, I was approached by a young woman offering me a store credit card. Have you noticed that the current spate of cold salespeople will never take "No thank you" for an answer? They always need to try to persuade you that you really do want/need their product and this day was no different. So I began to chat with this young woman. I told her I was against credit and felt that debt was ruining many lives. Her face changed from sales girl to young woman in trouble and she answered, "I have so much debt, I don't know how I will ever repay it. I, least of anyone, should be offering these cards." And she is not alone, a young man in our area had recently committed suicide, apparently because of debt. All his life to live, a good career, a girlfriend and a loving family but debt had stolen all this from him.

How have we reached the situation in the west, where we all want everything and we want it now? What we earn seems to bear no relation to what we spend. Do you remember the classic advice "Income: £20, outgoings: £20.10, unhappiness; income: £20, outgoings: £19.90, happiness."

Because I am so interested in lifestyle, I enjoy T.V. programmes that deal with life issues, including money. I am amazed at the level of denial of so many people in these programmes, who are deeply in debt. One young couple, already thousands of pounds in debt, (not even counting their mortgage), received excellent advice. Three months later they had done nothing to alleviate the situation, except buy a huge expensive dog. How much extra would he cost to feed each month?

Everywhere we turn we are offered credit and I understand how tempting it can be, I like beautiful things too. "Buy this settee, no payments for a year and 4 years free credit." "Buy this car, no deposit necessary." "Have this store card, 10% off your bill." "Consolidate your debts and have a few more thousands for a holiday or home improvements." About half the junk mail we receive offers yet another loan, another better credit card.

We have become as a nation greedy, materialistic, gullible, unwise and dishonest because many know the debt will not be repaid. Many have lost their peace of mind, self-esteem and the joy of owning what they have worked and saved for.

All this would be incredibly sad if it only affected those without God. After all, they don't have the joy and satisfaction that knowing Jesus brings. But unfortunately it is more than sad because this attitude has thoroughly infiltrated the church, we who know "we are strangers and pilgrims on this earth" Hebrews 11:13.

We who know to "store up for ourselves treasure in heaven where rust and moth cannot corrupt or thieves steal, because where our treasure is there will our heart be also" Matthew 6:20,21.

We who know, "seek first the kingdom of heaven and all that we need will be given to us." Matthew 6:34

We, too, have fallen into the enemy's trap of easy debt. Many of us have decided to adopt the world's standards and ignore God and the practical advice in His word.

Romans 13.8 tells us "Owe no one anything."
Hebrews 13:5 advises "not to covet but be content with what we have."
1 Timothy 6:6 "Godliness with contentment is great gain." Not found in a widescreen T.V. or latest video camera.

Proverbs 15:16 "Better is a little with the fear of the Lord than great treasure with trouble." Those huge bills each month, mostly interest!

I expect that many of us have at some time in our lives had a financial blip. The important thing is that we learn from our mistakes, deal with them, pay off our debts and become wiser.

As a young couple, David and I swapped our old Morris Minor convertible that had no heater, for a beautiful large, shiny, pale blue and chrome Ford Consul. I would probably think it rather vulgar now, but then we loved it. We had a loan to pay for it, plus it literally guzzled petrol. We had only owned this beautiful treasure for a few weeks when we realised it was only bringing us unhappiness. We swallowed our pride, sold it, and bought a small economical runabout. It was a hard lesson, but we learned it and have avoided debt all our married life. Owning even the most beautiful object will not bring happiness or self-worth, especially if we cannot afford it anyway. Have you noticed how quickly that coveted treasure becomes at best just one more possession and at worst an absolute burden?

While half the world starves and lives in abject poverty. The other half spends money they have not earned on possessions they do not need.

"Don't be obsessed with getting material things. Be relaxed with what you have. Since God assured us, "I'll never let you down, never walk off and leave you." Hebrews 13:11 (The Message)

What more can we want or covet than this?

Chapter 4
Glorify God In Your Body

This was my first article written for Joy after reading one about alcohol. And although the subject proved to be controversial, they invited me to continue writing for them, which I did for about five years.

Can I just stress, I am totally against the abuse of alcohol. Binge-drinking, drunkenness and associated behaviour is yet another scourge and the shame of this generation and as Christians, we do need to speak out and teach against such a lifestyle.

To enjoy a glass of wine with a meal is one thing, to abuse this and become influenced by alcohol is totally unacceptable. For many years David and I were teetotal because we were working amongst people who had alcohol-related problems. I have often thought that the teaching we received years ago of total abstinence made life so much simpler and if you should have any problems in this area, the best, safest and wisest response is still to abstain.

But alcohol is not the only place where abuse and greed occurs...

Reading the article about moderation with alcohol prompted me to write about something that often disturbs me. Especially in the light of recent media concentration on the dangers of obesity in the western nations becoming one of our greatest health problems. What should our attitude as Christians be to this present dilemma?

We almost never hear anyone mention the sin of gluttony or greed. I realise that these words could apply to several areas of our lives, sexual, money, power etc., but I am specifically talking about food.

So often we read of these sins in a list of what we consider more important, or more damaging or dangerous sins, immorality, sexual impurity, idolatry, slander, drunkenness, swindlers etc., 1 Corinthians 5:11.

But I suggest we cannot quote 1 Corinthians 6:19 "Your body is a temple of the Holy Spirit" to deter smokers and drug addicts as well as the immoral, while filling that same temple with so much fat, sugar and salt as to render it damaged.

So often in church life, we are faced with praying for the sick, very often long-term sick. We pray, we fast, we anoint, we lay hands on, and we weary ourselves praying with faith-destroying little results. And what I have so often noticed, not always of course, - not all fat people are sick and not all sick people are fat, - but often I have noticed that many of them are overweight or even obese. Leg joint pains, diabetes, blood pressure, heart problems, asthma and many more illnesses we are told, are exacerbated by excess weight.

Now hear me please, I'm not advocating that we should all be size 10-12 or waist 30". But we should seek to treat the body that God gave us with respect, eating moderately and healthily. If we want to live long, successful lives, serving God to the end, we need to have a body that is healthy enough to co-operate with our spirit. An overweight, unhealthy body hinders our service for God. It is also, I suggest, not a good testimony or example especially in this day and age.

I am a lifelong "almost vegetarian" and have at times had some leg pulling over this, "the weaker brother" etc. (Romans 14:12) But I believe that in the beginning, God gave fruit and vegetables to be eaten (Genesis 1:29-30) and only after the flood was meat eaten. Now hear me, I don't believe eating meat and fish is wrong (Acts 10:13-14), but God give us wisdom in how much we are consuming.

Isn't it interesting that so many of the things we are finding out today, God has known all along? - i.e. Fruit and vegetables are good for us, at least five portions a day regularly are strongly recommended.

I realise that to lose weight isn't easy and very much harder for some. Maintaining weight loss is even more tedious, especially as we get older! When I went through the menopause just a few years ago, I put on a stone in weight without really realising (no scales). I felt uncomfortable in my clothes and heavy. My knees and hips began to ache and I depressingly thought this was old age setting in. But over a period of a year, I lost 23lbs (very, very slowly), simply by cutting portions slightly and eating as healthily as I knew how. I was cutting back particularly on fat and sugar and eating loads of fruit, veg and salads. All my aches and pains disappeared.

My goal is to live a long, healthy and active life, serving God to the end, sucking the juice out of life and being a testimony for God. - To be able to prostrate myself before God if He tells me, and to dance before Him when prompted without needing medical intervention!

"Do you not know that your body is a temple of the Holy Spirit, who is in you, whom you have received from God? You are not your own, you were bought at a price. Therefore honour God with your body". 1 Corinthians 6:19-20

Excuse me while I make myself a salad sandwich. - On wholemeal of course!

Chapter 5
Choices

Every day each individual makes hundreds, perhaps thousands of choices. Some are indeed not very consequential, but many seemingly unimportant choices will affect our lives and the lives of the people around us, for potentially a very long time.

Each choice is like a pebble thrown into water and the ripples may be felt in an ever-widening circle of lives and time.

Many years ago, a young woman I knew made a choice to leave her husband. It was not meant to be permanent but was meant as a warning, perhaps a cry for help, it said, "I am unhappy, we need to change things." But circumstances conspired to make it impossible for her to return. The choice she made that day affected many, many lives and the repercussions are still felt today many years later.

Sometimes I listen to parents discouraged because their maturing children don't want to come to church. Raising children for Jesus is never easy in the world we live in today, many of us experience difficulties and my heart goes out to those struggling today. But to parents I would say, watch your choices. The decisions you make today with your children will affect them for years to come. If we are inconsistent and lukewarm in our church and spiritual lives, this is the example by which our children will be trained. If we only go to church when it's convenient and there's nothing else to do, the ripples will roll down through the years, potentially affecting the next generation.

The Bible says, "A fool messes up his life and blames God." Proverbs 19:3

How many times have we heard people blame God for things that have gone wrong in their lives when so often it is the choices made perhaps many years ago, and often repeatedly, that have done the damage.

Let me put it bluntly, choose to put your hand in the fire, you will burn. Choose to abuse your body, by say, smoking, you will get sick, perhaps not today or even tomorrow but choices bring consequences and we need to remember this.

We, who live in the west in the 21st century, have many choices, far more than any other generation before us. It is true to say that many areas of the world still do not have the choices in life that we enjoy. Still today people in much of the world, eat what is available, wear their only clothes, and never travel more than a few miles from their homes, just as it was even here in the U.K. not many generations ago. It must be said though, that having so much choice is a mixed blessing, especially if, like me, you can be a bit of a ditherer. Shopping can become a drawn-out nightmare as we are faced, not with simply a handful of options but with dozens or even hundreds.

From the moment our eyes open in the morning, decisions must be made. "Shall I have tea or shall I have coffee?" Not a very difficult choice, it really doesn't matter what we choose; our lives will not be affected in the slightest. There are many choices like this; we could almost toss a coin to decide. It is choices like this that we make every day, which if we make the same choice each time, will turn into a habit. If we are making a good choice, a good habit is formed, but conversely, if we choose unwisely, a bad habit is formed, which is extremely hard to break.

David is a very early riser; it is a choice he made a long time ago. It is his choice to have a time alone with God before his day really begins. Even on his day off, he is unable to sleep in. He has formed a good habit, it has become second nature to him, and little effort is involved.

But bad habits are unfortunately just as easy to form and take a great amount of willpower to change. When we are tired and can't be bothered to shop, cook and clear up, we turn to takeaways and junk food, don't we, but if we make this decision often enough, we become junk food addicts and extremely unhealthy. It becomes our norm and there is only one way to change the situation and that is to change our choices and keep changing them until the bad habit is broken. This, perhaps with more support, is how we give up smoking, alcohol and really any other addiction. Yes I know, not quite so easy as I make it sound, but what I want to get across is, an act of our will, a choice, is always needed to change bad habits in our lives, there is no magic wand.

I have heard it said that it takes 2-3 months of willpower before a choice becomes a habit or even before a bad habit is broken and things are not so difficult. I gave up sugar in drinks a few years ago and certainly, for a couple of months, tea and coffee were horrid, but then afterwards, when the habit was formed, I could no longer drink sweetened beverages.

Not all our choices are inconsequential and making a wrong decision will have huge repercussions that will harm our lives for some time. Who can today find their way through the money maze? Many years ago, I worked for a bank, but today the money system is a complete mystery to me and I think to most other people. What sort of account will be best for my money? Which mortgage will serve me best? Where will I get most interest for my savings? - A really difficult one today, - what about our pensions? To choose once is not enough either, we have to move our money around to get the best deals and to make the most of the bit of money we have. A wrong choice can cost us hundreds or even thousands of pounds.

Choosing our life partner is another area where if a wrong choice is made our whole life is affected. As Christians we choose for life, it is a one-off decision. I understand there are single people in the church who are almost desperate to have a partner and my heart goes out to them. A good marriage is a great blessing. But as I tell many who come to me in distress about their singleness, a bad marriage is horrendous. I always remember Paul Scanlon saying, "Being single is not a problem, being married to a nerd, now that's a problem!" Be warned, choose wisely, prayerfully and take your time. It is a life-changing decision; you will have a long time to regret it.

In our spiritual lives too, choices and our will play a major role, if we want successful and fulfilling lives. Many things that we often consider are feelings or a natural reaction is in fact a strong choice that certainly initially we make as an act of our will. If we keep making that choice, even in spiritual things, the choice becomes a habit and is easier and more natural, and our feelings do often eventually become involved.

To forgive is an act of our will, a choice. Unforgiveness can become a bad habit, which mars our lives. To worship is a choice we make, even when we don't feel like it, pretty soon our feelings catch up. To give, to submit, to honour, even to go to church are decisions, choices that form good habits in our lives that pay dividends spiritually. Yes, even the sort of Christians we are is our choice. In the story of Martha and Mary, it seems that Mary wasn't simply naturally the worshipper, the one who craved intimacy. The Bible tells us it was a choice she made, "Mary has chosen the better part". Luke 10:42

Many times when we fall into sin, it isn't simply one bad decision but a chain of tiny bad choices that we never correct and repent. Each bad choice gives more and more room to the enemy until he has us in his snare. No one gets up one morning from a happy and trusting marriage and decides to commit adultery. A catalogue of seemingly harmless choices leads us down the path of sin. If we are challenged we are offended and protest the innocence of the 'friendship'. If only we understood the power of temptation we, like Joseph, would 'flee' from the place of temptation.

And finally the greatest choice we will ever make in our lives, and God in his goodness has even given us choice in this. Joshua said to the children of Israel, "Choose this day whom you will serve, but as for me and my house, we will serve the Lord." Joshua 24:15

"I have set before you life and death, blessings and curses, now choose life." Deuteronomy 30:19

Choose life, choose Jesus.

Chapter 6
People

"People, people who need people, are the happiest people in the world."

And psychologists tell us the song is absolutely right, the happiest, healthiest people are those surrounded by friends and family. The serendipity of being a Christian is the blessing of belonging to a church family.

But although our friends bring us so much joy, pleasure and sense of well being, let's be brutally truthful, people are also our greatest pain and heartache. And in my role as a church pastor, inter-relational problems are probably the most common reason people seek support. In marriage, with our children, in-laws, friends, work colleagues and also within the church family, difficulties arise. We really shouldn't be too surprised or too upset about this and if handled properly, we can actually grow, mature and learn from the friction caused by "rubbing along" with other people and our relationships can become even deeper.

The Bible, among other things, is a book about people, people skills and problem-solving and has lots of advice about getting along with others, it's important that we don't just read this advice but apply it to our everyday relationships.

We know the Bible constantly commands us to love each other, but it is sometimes necessary to consider exactly how we can express this love.

This love is expressed by honouring, respecting and esteeming one another. (Romans 12:10 & Philippians:2.3) Dishonour and disrespect are catching. When we are disrespectful to friends and work colleagues, we invite disrespect back. It is even possible to honour and esteem our children or those under us. Even when correcting or disciplining, we can still show proper respect. It is perhaps important to say here, that equally important in relationships is self- respect. Respecting ourselves and insisting that others respect us too, is not only essential for us but for those around us. For example, the Bible tells children to honour their parents, (Ephesians 6.2.) it is part of our parental responsibility to teach our children to respect us. A disrespectful toddler may be amusing; a disrespectful teenager is embarrassing and even frightening.

Good manners, although out of date, are also, I believe, godly and a sign of honouring and loving. (1 Corinthians. 13:5) Giving up your seat to someone older or frailer, holding a door open, verbal manners such as, I am sorry, excuse me, please and thank you, are incredibly important in a relationship. I know they may seem trivial but they are not. They are a drop of calming oil between people. After all these years of marriage, David and I are careful to still maintain good manners with each other.

Another key to good relationships is encouragement. Whoever we are relating to, whether a small child or an older, mature person, sincere encouragement lubricates the wheels between us. Every one of us needs to hear from time to time, "Well done." It expresses, "I am for you, I notice what you are doing, I acknowledge and appreciate your gifting." If we just think of the opposite, discouragement, we would understand just how vital it is to have those we associate with encouraged. An encouraged child is a happier, better-behaved child. An encouraged husband or wife wants to please and bless their spouse and put even more effort into the relationship. This encouragement can be carried through all our relationships to great positive effect; even your boss in work needs to be encouraged.

And there are so many other virtues between people that God in His word encourages. Kindness, (Ephesians 4:32) don't be harsh with those around but be kind, gentle and tender-hearted.

"A soft answer" the Bible says, "turns away wrath" and when we bless those who hurt us, we cause them to regret their animosity. (Proverbs 15:1 & Romans 12:20)

Compromise is also important. No two people, even in marriage, will feel exactly the same about an issue. Ask yourself, "Is this particular issue really that important?"

Don't let us be easily offended, such people are incredibly wearing to be around and if we do get hurt in the general hustle and bustle of life, let forgiveness flow. But should we hurt someone else, - take responsibility; let our apology be sincere and full.

Loyalty is another issue. Disloyalty and gossiping about others is not only a heartbreaker but also a relationship breaker. Wise women don't destroy their own family and marriage with their tongue, (Proverbs 14:1) and this applies to all our friendships, build up and do not pull down.

God hates quarrelling, discord, disunity and divorce and where we set our hearts and determine to make every effort to live at peace with others, - in our home, our workplace, the church, or where ever we are, - there God promises to bestow His blessing. (Psalm 133)

Chapter 7
Surviving The Credit Crunch

How very suddenly and for most of us, unexpectedly, the recent credit crisis fell upon us.

Those of us who are "comfortable" are suddenly and disturbingly, a little less so and those of us who just make ends meet, or are in financial difficulties already, are now in crisis.

It is often at such a time when we are forced to take stock of our lifestyle choices that an apparent curse can become, in God, a tremendous blessing and a power for good in our lives.

David and I have always sought to live, even our financial lives, with the word of God as our guide. I should perhaps confess here that we have no idea how to "wheel and deal" and are extremely naïve in our approach to money. However, in our defence, let me say that in all our varying levels of wealth, we have never been in debt, never had an unpaid bill and for the last twenty years have owned outright our home in one of the villages of East Yorkshire. All attributed to the blessing, timing and goodness of our God.

Here is our five-point guide to financial freedom.

First of all the Bible encourages us to work. "The man who doesn't work shouldn't eat" (2 Thessalonians 3:10). Benefits should never be a chosen lifestyle but are there to see us through the bad times, when we are genuinely unable to work or if in spite of real diligent effort, we cannot find a job. (Can I just say here, "living by faith" to serve God does not mean living on benefits!)

Secondly and crucially, giving at least one-tenth of our income into the local church, where we are being fed and nurtured, (Malachi 3:10). This we believe is the key to financial and lifestyle blessing, take the ten per cent right off the top as our first and most pressing financial responsibility. Our experience is, the 90% goes further with God than the 100% goes without Him.

Some years ago our older son, Jason, was out of work for one winter and had to sign on for benefits. Occasionally he managed to acquire a couple of days casual work in the Lake District, so he would sign off and sign on again the next week, (It would have been very easy not to bother with this but, integrity is another key to God's blessing in our finances.) One Sunday, all he had in his wallet was his tithes, but that coming week had a little work over in Cumbria and needed the money for train fare. But during the meeting, he heard God tell him to pay his tithes. He and God had a little discussion, but God insisted, "Give me the money that is due." Jason obeyed and paid the tithes. As we pulled out of the car park later on that morning, I saw Jason pull a brown envelope out of his pocket, open it and burst out laughing, There God's special gift to him was three times what he had given in the offering. God is indeed no man's debtor. Honour and obey God and He will bless.

Our third point is to pray about our finances, committing the 90% to Him. Asking God to bless, multiply and give us wisdom in how we spend. Big purchases are certainly prayed over and even things as trivial as the housekeeping, especially on a heavy financial week, will be specifically brought under His blessing.

Fourthly, live by a budget. Learn to be a little economical. It doesn't hurt us to have to understand that even when under God's blessing we cannot have everything. Ask God for wisdom. For example, even after praying over the housekeeping, it may be wise when things are tight, to steer away from the best steak, salmon, asparagus and Scottish raspberries, unless of course they are on offer, which is a regular occurrence and blessing!

And finally, and this advice will potentially change the course of your financial life, cut up your credit cards. They are not for the poor or those just making ends meet, they are for the rich. Unless you are able to pay them off completely each month, your hard earned cash will line the pockets of the banks. My other objection to them is that it becomes easier to trust the credit card to meet our immediate need than to trust in God.

A newly married couple in our church needed a dining table and chairs. They looked around the appropriate shops and decided they couldn't afford one without going into debt and this they didn't want to do. Two weeks later, a relative phoned and offered them a beautiful dining suite they no longer needed. Here is the choice, trust the credit card and be in debt or trust God and have testimonies to share.

In feast or famine, Jehovah Jireh, our God will provide if we let Him.

Chapter 8
Success

We live in an age of celebrity, an age when many of our young people if asked their aspirations, will reply, "I want to be rich and famous." If one digs deeper and asks in what area do they wish to succeed? Do they want to play a sport, be a musician, an actor, a scientist or even a minister? Many of them will respond, "I just want to be a celebrity".

Much of "reality" T.V. has fed this unhealthy desire in our young, when ordinary unknowns have their 15 minutes of fame. It seems the more outrageous, crass, vulgar and cruel they are in front of the cameras, the greater the fame. It also seems to have become a pattern, especially in the media, that as professional careers deteriorate, a little of this type of exposure revitalises things and aids apparent success. Impressionable young minds now have as their role models and heroes, men and women with deeply disturbed and troubled lives, where no amount of money and fame brings the peace, joy, satisfaction and love they crave.

Many of these celebrities live a life dependent on drugs and alcohol. They move from one unsatisfactory relationship to another, damaging the lives of the children these relationships produce. Is this the type of success to which our young people, in the church and in the nation, ought to aspire?

I have never been a very driven person and have never aspired to fame, riches and power. In fact, I think I can truthfully say, I have a fairly contented character and realised long ago that although these things may be a blessing, they potentially also carry a curse.

But in spite of this, I do have a deep desire to be successful and, in fact, like so many people, I hate the thought of failure.

David and I had been in ministry for many years, but we had never heard any other minister admit to struggles and failures until we attended a special leaders conference. A middle-aged French Pastor stood and wept before us all, as he recounted past struggles, failures and church splits before he finally knew success. How very sincere, honest, real and vulnerable we found him.

Some years ago, our church in Hull was going through tough times and I particularly felt the pressure of this. I clearly remember spending a Monday morning on my face before God, crying out to Him about my fear of failure. I was fearful that New Life Church would not fulfil the destiny spoken over her. I was fearful for our church family and how failure would perhaps stumble the weaker and less mature and I was afraid to fail the city where God had called us. And in all truth, I did not want the humiliation that I believed failure might bring.

Just as many women do, I was quick to lay much of the blame at our feet. If only we were stronger, more spiritual, more pastoral, more mature, more loving and patient, more evangelical, more gifted, more anything!

During the weeks before this distressed prayer time, three different, unconnected people had given us Zechariah 4:6. "Not by might, nor by power but by my Spirit, says the Lord Almighty."

On this particular Monday, David, knowing nothing of my current anguish, came home in the evening and said, "You know that scripture that God has given us three times, well I read it today in the Good News Translation, and do you know what it says?"

"You will succeed, not by military might or by your own strength, but by my spirit."

With tears of joy, I shared my earlier fears and pain and praised God for all His comfort and reassurance. We would not fail, in fact God says, we will succeed, not because of us but because of Him. I continue to this day to repeat this promise regularly over my marriage, family, ministry, church and myself.

The Bible is not against success, there is no virtue in failure, unless we use it to learn, grow and finally succeed. Success is a really valid and wonderful aspiration. Succeed in education, in music, in sport, in the arts, succeed in your careers, and succeed in your ministry, in your family, in your health and finances. But above all, measure success in Kingdom terms.

2 Chronicles 26:4-5 says, "Uzziah did what was right in the eyes of the Lord…As long as he sought the Lord, God gave him success."

Proverbs 16:3, "Commit to the Lord whatever you do and your plans will succeed."

And my prayer for you is Psalm 20. Paraphrased, "May the Lord answer you, may He protect you and help you and grant you support, May He remember you, May He give you the desires of your heart and make all your plans succeed."

SECTION 2

Dealing With Rubbish In Our Lives

Chapter 9
When It's Alright To Be Angry
Part 1

We live in an angry and violent world. Road rage and violent assaults on people are common, everyday occurrences. Even our emergency services, the very people to whom we should show deep gratitude and appreciation, are not immune from such attacks. Our nations' obsession with alcohol only fuels the problem. As Christians, we abhor such out of control emotions that lead to so much pain. The Bible also tells us not to give way to anger. (Colossians 3:8)

But anger is not always sinful and harmful. There is a right anger that can lead to liberty and wholeness in our lives. It does not destroy; it builds up and brings life. It is not an out of control emotion, but a spirit controlled response to evil.

In John 2:13-16 is a wonderful, colourful story of a day when Jesus got really angry. Traders within the temple were apparently defrauding and robbing the worshippers in the selling of sacrificial animals and changing money. Jesus was having none of it, - made a whip and drove them out. He gave them no alternative and accepted no excuses, his Fathers' temple was no place to steal and defraud. How many before him had seen the problem, moaned about it, even half-heartedly complained, but didn't see it through? Jesus' anger was controlled, directed at the right source and carried through to completion.

1 Corinthians 3:16 says that we are the temple of God and again in 1 Corinthians 6:19 it says our body is the temple of God. Why do we allow our enemies to rob, defraud and spoil our lives by the illegitimate businesses they establish in our personal 'temple' of Gods spirit? Whether it is the appetites and habits of our own flesh, the pressure and brain-washing of our world, or Satan and the demonic, when they seek to establish themselves in our lives and rob us of everything Jesus has for us, they are our enemies and we should deal with them as Jesus dealt with these "bricks and mortar" temple traders.

Let's look at a few steps we can take to spiritually make a whip and drive the enemy from our temple. First of all, we need to acknowledge there is a problem. So often we are accepting of less than God's best for our lives and think it is inevitable and we have to accept and live with a situation. Let me give you an example that illustrates how I accepted less than God's best for my life.

Almost all my adult life, every month, I suffered from 3-4 day migraine type headaches. Of course I prayed about them, but I reasoned, I was a woman and had hormones. I prided myself on coping with them, never cancelling appointments or letting anyone down, although the painkillers may have glazed my eyes a little! I've reached the age now where every hormone has left this body and I no longer suffer! But how I regret accepting and permitting, this in my life for so long.

If you have any long-term problem, I in no way want to condemn you, on the contrary, I want to encourage you to stand and fight anew for release in this area of your life. I realise that discouragement, disappointment and even embarrassment that "people will think I don't have enough faith", comes into our lives when prayer isn't answered immediately, but this is the devil talking isn't it? John 10:10 says that Jesus came to give us abundant life and I believe that anything that prevents this abundance from happening in our lives is less than God's best for us and is a problem.

Secondly, decide with every sinew of your being, I will NOT have this in my life. Sometimes this determination is only triggered when Satan pushes us just one step too far and thankfully we make that all important decision, "so far enemy, but no farther". This happened to me when my children were teenagers in Gibraltar and I had sensed them pulling away from God. It came to a head one mid-week meeting when the guest speaker called all the youth forward for prayer. My older son was not even in church and my younger son, on hearing the appeal, shot out of the church, leaving the keyboard he was playing, as if the devil himself was in pursuit. I ran out to the church kitchen and began to sob. When some of the women followed me, all I could say was "My children, my children." I thank God for that night because a new determination rose up in me, that the enemy would not, not, not have my children. I resumed with renewed enthusiasm that "effectual fervent prayer" that will eventually bring results.

Thirdly, we need to recognise again the authority within us to bind, drive out, reject and refuse these negatives in our lives. Remember Jesus made a whip and drove them out, allow him to be our example and let us accept no excuses the enemy offers, such as, "You are getting older your health is bound to suffer." "All teenagers are trouble." "Everyone is in debt." "You've been married 20 years, you're not supposed to still love your husband." "Your mother had it, it's hereditary." These are all lies of the enemy, whoever that enemy is, - the world, the flesh or the devil and not to be accepted. And should the devil say you are not strong enough, 1 John 4:4 says, "The one who is in you, is greater than the one who is in the world." And to emphasise our authority, 1 John 3:8 reminds us that Jesus broke the power of Satan on our behalf.

Jesus died not just to free us from sin, shame, death and hell but sickness, poverty, anxiety and depression, to give us an abundant and joyful life, to turn every curse into a blessing.

Chapter 10
When It's Alright To Be Angry
Part 2

Having ousted the negative, next let's bless our lives with the positive. As Christians we believe in the power of blessing don't we, blessing our city, our church, our children and our lives. And although if we only said "God bless me and mine", it would be a selfish prayer, in right balance, it is a wonderful prayer, bringing into our lives all that God has for us and, by the way, being a wonderful testimony to those around us when they see God's hand in our lives, bringing us through our trials. Do you remember the prayer of Jabez that so touched our hearts a few years ago, (1 Chronicles 4:10) "Oh God that you would bless me indeed and enlarge my territory," and from a negative beginning and a negative name, Jabez means pain, the Bible simply says, "And God granted his request." God bless us with health, body, soul and spirit; prosperity, enough to live and to give; a united Christian family and a loving marriage.

And then speak the word of God over our lives, appropriating His eternal promises.

"As are your days so shall your strength be," (Deut 33:25) one of my favourites recently!

"By his stripes, I am healed," (Isaiah 53:5) I'm struggling with a sciatic nerve right at this moment.

"The Joy of the Lord is my strength," (Neh 8:10)

"I can do all things through Christ who strengthens me." (Phil 4:13) There's too much sadness and weakness in our world.

And "Jehovah Jireh, my Provider." (Gen 22:14)

I remember that great man of God, Derek Prince saying he and his wife took the word of God at least three times a day as a medicine, speaking it over their lives to bring health and wholeness.

The next step for us, is to ask God, "What must I do to obtain and appropriate the answer to my prayers?" Because although God will bring the answer, the Holy Spirit requires our co-operation and this action may be in one or two ways. It may be by a prophetic act, something seemingly senseless or useless. Remember when Naaman had to dip seven times in Jordan? (2 Kings 5) Did the dipping cure him of his leprosy? No, his obedience did. What about when the children of Israel needed water and Moses struck the rock, was there water in the rock? No, of course not, Moses' obedience brought the answer. A modern example, some months ago I told you about a childless woman in our church who was told to sing and rejoice a child into her life (from Isaiah 54). Did singing cause conception? No, obedience did. God says do you have faith to obey a seemingly useless instruction? When we do, it says, I believe, I have faith in my God, and as we all know faith moves mountains.

But conversely, God may tell us to do something very wise, to have wisdom in the way we live in order to obtain or even to keep our answers to prayer, our miracles. For example, to receive and keep your healing, live healthily, live wisely. To stay out of debt, stop spending unnecessarily, cut up credit cards, draw up a budget and get help if necessary.

For a strong marriage and family, give time, patience, love and respect. The word of God is full of advice, remember the enemy is against marriage and family and we see evidence of this all around us. It is possible to hinder, delay or even lose our miracle by the unwise way in which we live. Repentance for our previous lifestyle may be a key in our release.

Perseverance is our next key to wholeness. We live in a speed orientated world, microwave meals, e-mails, speed dialing, fast travel, but God says persevere in prayer.

Ask and keep on asking, knock and keep knocking, seek and keep seeking and you will receive, is the fuller meaning in Matthew 7.7. And again in Luke 11:5 and 18:1 are stories Jesus told to encourage us to persist, don't give up, endure and you will see a change, an answer. We prayed at least 2-3 years for our sons walk with God. We prayed a year for an answer to a neck problem before the healing came. We prayed for seven years for a dear friend with a chronic, degenerative illness. Persist - the answer will come.

And finally, when that release comes, reach out for it, grab it with both hands, stand in God and hold on to it, refuse to let it go, because, take notice, the enemy will want to steal it again. Then tell us about Gods goodness in your life with a heart of gratitude, praise and testimony. It increases our faith to believe for our own miracle. Romans 10:17 says "Faith comes by hearing." Let us hear your astounding testimony so we can believe for ours. And watch out for the blessings. Proverbs 6:31 says if anyone steals from us, he must restore sevenfold.

And God says "I will restore the years the locust has eaten". Joel 2:25 Watch out, here come blessings.

Chapter 11
We Are Not Ignorant Of His Devices

My spiritual background, which I embrace, taught me not to dwell on the activities of the enemy, but on the power, glory and work of our God. However, 2 Corinthians 2:11 exhorts us "not to be oblivious of his sly ways" (MSG)

And the other week, an unusual dream caused me some thought. A couple of years ago we accompanied Jarrod and Vicky on a ministry trip to South Africa. While there we visited the Kruger Game Reserve. It was a wonderful time and my dream recalled one of our experiences there.

I dreamt we were all safely in the car but were being stalked by a large male lion. I became concerned that one of us would get out of the car and be attacked. I awoke urging my family, "Don't get out of the car!" The next morning over breakfast, much to David's bewilderment, I urged him, "If ever we go to Kruger again, don't get out of the car, will you?"

I soon realised my dream may hold a spiritual warning. In the game reserve, while you remain in the car you are totally safe, the lion cannot touch you. It is important to remain in the car at all times because lions are extremely well camouflaged. When we eventually saw one, we realised we may have passed several without ever seeing them.

Our enemy, the Bible says, prowls around as a roaring lion seeking whom he may devour. (1 Peter 5:8) Just as I urged my family in that dream, I urge you, "Stay in the car, take no risks." Our spiritual "car" is that secure place of living and walking in the centre of God's will. When we walk in sin and disobey His word, we remove ourselves from that safe place of His protection and we potentially give the enemy a foothold in our lives. When Jason worked with Aid Agencies in war zones, he would only go when he knew he was in God's will, then no matter the threat, he knew he was safe and protected.

This dream led me to think about other adventures in the game reserve that may also hold spiritual warnings. One evening we were leaving our lodge to walk across the camp to the restaurant. Vicky, my daughter-in-law, was the first to walk down the lodge steps. Suddenly I heard a tiny shriek and she turned and began to push us all back inside, warning us "Get back, there's a snake!" There, on the steps, barely visible in the dusk, was a small brown snake. Vicky had initially thought it was a silk scarf and had almost bent to pick it up. Only slightly shaken, Jarrod got on his mobile to reception and asked for a ranger. I was convinced it was only a grass snake. When the ranger came, he informed us it was a puff adder, the biggest killer snake in Africa! Apparently, it appears deceptively slow, calm and harmless, but when you get close, its strike is like lightning and its venom deadly.

How like our enemy. So often Satan, the seducer, appears harmless, even attractive, and we make the mistake of consorting with him. When he appeared to Eve, if he had been seen as ugly, evil, dangerous, with the potential to cause the downfall of mankind, would she have listened, and talked with him? I think not.

At times, Satan seeks to enter our lives, not as a roaring, devouring lion, but with subtlety and cunning. He whispers in our ear, "This isn't bad or dangerous, it's interesting and harmless, and everyone does it." I remember as a young woman reading horoscopes in women's magazines, believing them harmless fun until God strongly convicted me I was playing with the enemy. Satan is not a silk scarf or a harmless grass snake, he is a liar, a thief, an accuser and a destroyer, beware.

Another morning, we had just left camp, when we came across a huge bull elephant. We stopped the car to watch as he crossed the road in front of us. In crossing, he noticed our car and, being in a bad mood that morning, decided he did not want us there. Tossing his head, shaking his huge ears and raising his trunk, he began to pursue us. David was at the wheel and the rest of us began to yell, "Reverse, reverse!" Still trying to watch the elephant, David reversed only to hit the verge. He then had to drive towards the angry elephant to release us! That elephant pursued us almost back to camp.

Sometimes our enemy, the intimidator, doesn't like where we are and what we have in God and he begins, like a rampaging elephant, to drive us backwards. He brings annoyances into our life; he touches our health, our relationships, our children and our ministry. In the game reserve, we were willing to reverse all the way back to camp to appease the elephant, it was, after all, his territory, but that is not how to deal with Satan. If we give ground, he will demand and take even more, if we retreat, he will advance. But instead, let us be strong in the Lord, stand our ground and with the sword of the Spirit in one hand and the shield of faith in the other, protected head to foot in the armour of God, and declare, " So far enemy and no further." (Ephesians 6:10-18) Stand and protect your health, your finances, your marriage and family; stand for your church, your city and your nation.

No matter the guise that Satan uses, whether as the devouring lion, the seducing snake or like the elephant that intimidates, we are exhorted to "stand against his wiles".

Be encouraged, Jesus came "that He might destroy the works of the devil" 1 John 3:8

And, "He who is in you is greater than he who is in the world."

Chapter 12
Spring: Clear The Clutter

Do you ever watch, 'How Clean is your House'? It's a T.V. programme about people who live in an appalling mess and they have found that the worse it gets the harder it is to tackle. Eventually, they, or a friend or relative, call in this team of cleaners headed by two strong ladies who clean up their mess. The mess affects every part of their lives, dressing, cooking, entertaining, even the children won't bring friends home because of embarrassment. But it isn't just that there is a mess, hidden in the confusion of dirty clothes and unwashed dishes, we discover there are hidden, unseen germs that could make this family ill or potentially kill them. The parents often cry at realising the danger in which they have put their family.

And when the house is cleaned up, they cry again because they hadn't realised how beautiful their home was under all the rubble! An added bonus is that often some precious object will be rediscovered, such as a filthy old vase turns out to be a real antique, making the hard work all that more worthwhile.

Now, much as I tried, I couldn't find a scripture that says, "cleanliness is next to godliness". And here I am not so much talking about physical cleaning as spiritual, but I realised many parallels can be drawn.

It's almost spring again. The days are getting longer and the sun has just a little bit more warmth. The gardens are filling with colour, and the shops are stocked with lighter clothes. I love this time of year because it brings the promise of summer, of long, warm days in the garden, of shedding heavy clothing, of picnics. I know that in Great Britain this promise is not always fulfilled.

We, in Hull, are still recovering from the terrible floods of last summer (2007), but nevertheless, we still hope in spring, that summer will come.

Another reason I love spring is spring-cleaning. It's not so much the cleaning as the de-cluttering that really exhilarates me. I love going through my wardrobe and getting rid of everything that no longer fits, is tired and shabby, or is simply too out of date to use again. Too many of us, especially after a certain age, have wardrobes bursting at the seams with clothes that we no longer wear. But because we have so many already, we're reluctant to buy something up to date and flattering for us today.

The same goes for our cupboards and storerooms. Why do we hold on to so much unused, unnecessary junk? We have complicated kitchen equipment, gathering dust because we would rather use a fork or a wooden spoon. [They're so much easier to clean afterwards.] And what about the unused gym gear, the exercise bike cluttering up the bedroom and now used as a hanging rail?

When I'm in spring-cleaning mode, David holds on to his chair, just in case I decide he's no longer necessary. I reassure him, "I'm getting rid of everything that is not beautiful or useful." Fortunately, he still fits into the "useful" category! I suggest he gets "useful" in the garage and throws away just some of the bits and pieces he thinks he might just use at some time in the future.

I don't know what makes me feel this way, perhaps it's because I've moved nations twice and know what a burden too many possessions can be. I just know de-cluttering makes me feel light-hearted and liberated. (There's no need to throw things in the bin, let a charity shop benefit.)

But more importantly, it is a good thing to spring clean and de-clutter our spiritual lives. Just as a wardrobe jam-packed with old clothes that are no longer appropriate, prevents us buying fresh clothes and looking good today, a life jam-packed with emotional baggage or old ministry commitments, prevents us from moving forward in God and embracing new challenges.

I'm a great believer in commitment and consistency, yet many of our ministries have run their course, but we become possessive and cling on to them for too long. It hinders us from moving out of our old comfort zones, advancing to new responsibilities and stretching ourselves.

In de-cluttering, even spiritually, the questions are similar, "Is this still useful and appropriate for me today?"

And, of course, the most important question, what is God saying about this? Is He saying – "Hang in there, keep going!"

Or is He saying, "It's been good and fruitful, but now it's over."

Or perhaps even "Hand it over to someone else, allow them to bring new vision and direction."

God will then lead you into fresh areas. While we hold on to the old, the familiar, the comfortable, we can't move on to the new, the exciting and the adventurous.

I am so linked into ministering to the church, that during a recent emphasis on reaching out to the City, I had a real crisis about where I could fit in with evangelism. All my time, energy and thought was going into nurturing the church family. I verbalised this quandary I felt I was in and it took my daughter-in-law to say, "What do you mean, you will talk to absolutely anyone. We're not in a coffee shop 5 minutes and you're either talking to the people at the next table or the waitress." And the penny dropped. I did have something to contribute to this current emphasis, although I hadn't been using it too much recently, I could chat and when appropriate, I could chat Jesus. Too much clutter in our spiritual lives can prevent us seeing exactly what we do have and when the clutter is removed; we often discover a forgotten treasure or dormant gifting.

God told Gideon, "Go in the strength you have," Joshua 6:14. Sometimes we need to de-clutter to see that strength in our lives so that God can lead us into new adventures in Him.

Another sensitive area to seriously pray about de-cluttering is relationships. At times in my life, I have had friends who have undermined who I am, my relationship with God, other friends and loved ones. I have usually stayed in these relationships for all the right reasons, - to help, encourage and support. But there comes a de-cluttering moment when we have to realise that not everyone wants to grow in God, put the past behind them and become the 'sons' God intended.

Of course, these are human beings that God loves, but a handful of times in my life, I have had to make a conscious decision to limit my time and commitment to people who, rather than I encouraging them, they are discouraging me. It doesn't prevent us blessing and praying, it just establishes boundaries on our contact.

Many of us also carry emotional baggage in our lives that weighs us down and prevents us from 'taking off' in God. Sometimes we carry this baggage for many years and never quite find the time to spiritually deal with it. Before we know it, the baggage builds up until we are paralysed by the weight of our past, old hurts, past failures and rejections.

Even old familiar sins and habits, things we know are wrong and not good for us, we accept because we believe nothing can change. We've tried in the past and failed, so we've come to accept our limitations, we've become comfortable in our weakness. It's often good to de-clutter with a trusted friend, someone who will tell you the truth, - in love, of course!

"No matter how expensive that coat was, it makes you look enormous."

Nowhere is this principle truer than when we are seeking to deal with a "besetting sin," – something that over a long period of time, regularly trips us up. A confidante to hold us accountable, to pray with us, to be our support system, not to judge us, but to encourage us, "You can do it", and with God, we can be overcomers.

Some of the habitual sins in our lives, we have become comfortable with. We reason that God is still blessing us, we are still able to operate in our ministries therefore we are coping with, what we realise is a less than perfect situation. But just as in physical mess there are often hidden germs that will potentially harm, so in our spiritual 'mess' there are hidden dangers.

David and I once knew a gifted young man. He was already in a place of spiritual responsibility and it was obvious to all of us that he was "going places" in God. But hidden from all our view he had a habit that went unchecked. He was hooked into pornography. I'm sure he believed he was coping with this weakness, but this sin gave a foothold to Satan and in time the young man committed adultery, destroying his marriage and family and also his ministry.

Song of Songs 2:15 says, "Catch for us the foxes, the little foxes that ruin the vineyards, our vineyards that are in bloom." It is the little things, the small besetting sins, the unchecked habits that steal our destiny. We all sin, this is for sure, but Psalm 66 talks about the danger of "Regarding sin in our lives" (means: - looking at and not dealing with).

And God, in His mercy, has given us two all-purpose, incredibly effective cleaning agents; there is nothing in our lives that these cannot deal with. The first is God's Word. Why do we encourage all believers to regularly read it, meditate on it, and study it? Because John 17:17 says, "Purify them with your truth, your word is truth." Even when we are unaware of benefiting from reading the Bible, it is cleansing us, convicting us, challenging us and changing our thought patterns, making us more like Jesus.

The second all-powerful cleanser is the blood of Jesus Christ. When applied in faith to our lives and our sin, we are clean. 1 John 1:8-9 says, "If we confess our sins, he is faithful and just and will forgive us our sins and purify us from all unrighteousness."

Understand this, the worst sinner who has ever lived, if they had applied the sacrifice Jesus made on the cross by the shedding of His blood, to their lives, they would be clean, forgiven, God's child. It has nothing to do with the gravity of the sin but all to do with the power of the blood. From this, I therefore understand there is nothing in my life or yours that cannot be freely cleansed! Praise God!

What does Hebrews 12 say? – "Let us strip off every weight that slows us down, especially the sin that so easily hinders our progress."

Spring is the season to call "time" on the darkness, heaviness, dormancy and cold of winter and to prepare our lives, our hearts, and our spirits for summertime, - A time of sunshine and warmth, of growth and fruitfulness.

Song of Songs 2:11 "See the winter is past, The rains are over and gone, flowers appear on the earth, the time of the singing of the birds has come, the cooing of doves is heard in our land".

But while we are thinking about de cluttering and spring cleaning our lives, let's just consider a couple of other areas that so often become messy and we accumulate unwanted debris. The first area is our attitudes.

Life throws so much into our path that it is easy to pick up wrong attitudes. Initially, we may have had every reason to feel this way. But negative feelings in our lives need dealing with or very quickly we become overwhelmed and life and ministry are affected. Such things as moaning, negativity, contrariness, unforgiveness, (see the chapter on unforgiveness.) lack of team spirit, nit-picking, rebellion, all negatively affect who we are and undermine our power in Jesus. Even sickness can be an attitude that pervades our lives. We may experience several sicknesses and if we don't check our thinking instead of being a person who is sick, we become a sick person. Do you see the difference? We begin to expect and sometimes even live and have our identity in our illnesses. The Bible says, "As a man thinks, so is he." (Proverbs 23:7) Our thinking affects our lives. If I believe I am sick, I will be sick. I know this is simplifying things a little, but even psychologists today line themselves up, unwittingly, with the Bible and say our attitude does indeed affect our lives.

One area God has been convicting me is in cynicism. I never intended to become this way, but many problems early on in both the churches we have led, caused me to become distrusting of people. They may verbalise love, commitment and loyalty, but inside, underneath my smile, I am secretly thinking, "Oh yes and for how long?" God has been showing me, this wall I built around my heart to protect myself against hurt and perhaps for very sound reasons, now is the time to pull it down. This, God tells me, is a different day and I need to trust again. What do you need to remove in your attitudes that are holding you back?

The final area where clutter prevents our best is in our time. Time is our most precious commodity and it is the place where the vast majority of us feel pressure. Life presses in on us and demands our time and it is an area where we definitely need to take control and not allow circumstances to rule. Time is the most precious thing we can give those we love. Marriages fail, children rebel, friendships are weak and God seems distant, all because of lack of time. It seems in my life, that whoever or sometimes whatever, shouts the loudest gets my time - and this is not right. Let's prioritise and give time to that which is most precious, most important and most fruitful in our lives. Leisure is important, but not when it steals from our God. When we regularly choose to stay home and watch a "soap" rather than go to the prayer meeting, we are wasting our time. Money is essential, but when we work all hours God sends rather than be with our spouse and our children, we are missing the mark.

God give us wisdom with our time and to know balance in our lives. We need time for our families, time for God Himself, time for ministry, time for our work and education, for our friends, for the church. And do you know what? - Time for ourselves. I want to enjoy the journey, to take time to smell the roses, to walk along a beach with my husband, to spend time with Jesus asking Him for nothing but simply enjoying His presence.

Colossians 4:5 talks of redeeming the time, making the most of every opportunity, God help us to do just that and not at the end of our lives, as we lay on our deathbeds, be full of regret, knowing that we got it wrong and used our time and our energy in the wrong areas.

Chapter 13
Who Am I?

In our home, we have several mirrors, we don't live in the largest house and we consider them a good interior design feature. But I must be truthful and say that the mirrors are also there because we are quite a vain family and check our image fairly regularly! Some days I am quite happy with what is reflected there and think I have worn fairly well. But I have my days when I deeply regret having so many reflections around me. There in the mirror is my dear mother, I look old and tired, and my self-confidence takes a serious battering on such days.

I wonder when you look in the mirror what you see? Are you comfortable with your image or do you lack self-esteem? How strange that we can interpret what we see in so many ways. What happens between the reflection in the mirror, our eyes and our brain? Just yesterday, I was talking to a beautiful young woman, her skin glows, her hair is blond and shiny, she is slim but curvy and her vibrant character shines through her eyes. She is married to a man she adores and who loves her too, she has a child and an interesting job, yet she tells me she lacks confidence in her appearance and who she is as a woman. Who or what is distorting her perception? And we can look deeper than merely our physical appearance; let's look inside ourselves, at our past, our character, our education and achievements, our relationships and friendships. Who do we see when we look into this "mirror"? Again it is all too easy to concentrate on the negatives, our past mistakes and failures, broken relationships, basic education, lack of finance, flawed character, - too old, too young.

At such times we have a choice of who to believe, what image to accept. We can believe the world, which says you are unacceptable unless you are size eight or below, unless your skin is flawless and your hair bouncy, which feeds us all airbrushed photos and says, aspire to this. The world who says we have to have it all or we have failed, a fantastic marriage, perfect children, a brilliant career, expensive possessions, at least one university degree and a strong, yet warm and charming character!

We may choose to believe the flesh and trust our own fickle judgement. I've told you, one day I'm moderately attractive (for my age!), yet another day I wish I could put a paper bag over my head - and I'm not just talking physically here, this fickleness affects what I feel about the inner me, too.

We can believe the enemy, who is a thief, a liar and an accuser. His only aim is to make us believe we are one ugly, useless, weak person.

Or we can choose to believe our heavenly Father, our God and our King. When I was a little girl, I used to dream I was a changeling, a princess, accidentally deposited in a working-class home and one day I would be reclaimed by my real Father, the King. I grew up to realise this was indeed the truth and that my "real" Father is not just a King, but the King of Kings and this is who He says I am. He says and I quote, that I am beautiful, loved and precious, the apple of His eye. I am forgiven and accepted and not timid, in fact, I have the spirit of love, power and a sound mind. I am chosen from before creation, a joint heir with Christ, with unlimited access to God my Father. I have the power to bind and loose and to move mountains; in fact, I am able to do greater works than Jesus. I am safe and protected against all enemies and calamities, holy and righteous with a secure future, part of a royal priesthood with the power to bless, heal and deliver. I am rich, healthy and possess every spiritual blessing and in spite of my gender, I am a royal prince, having power with God and man. My past is behind, dealt with, indeed I am a new creation. I have everything I need for life and godliness and I participate in the divine nature of Christ. As a citizen of heaven, I have a guaranteed inheritance, I know the truth and it has set me free. And that is only a tiny part of who I am.

If you suffer in any way with your image, not just physical, but emotional and spiritual, I challenge you over the next few months, to read God's word and to listen to every message, asking, "Who does God say I am in Jesus?" And choose to believe Him.

Chapter 14
Compromise

Compromise is one of those strange paradoxical words that can either be a huge positive and oil the wheels of human relationships or a huge negative and the thin end of the wedge in causing massive division.

The Church of England is right now, as I write, in the midst of critical negotiations, brought about by compromise, that realistically it cannot win. Whatever outcome is the result of these discussions, huge sections of our national church will be sufficiently disillusioned and distressed to call time on their church affiliation.

As they discuss, particularly the appropriateness of the appointment of homosexual bishops, let us be warned that compromising on God's word is never successful, never really appeases the rebel or the opinionated and effectively removes God and His Holy Spirit from the equation. The moment we begin to put human desires, opinions and current fashionable trends, over or even equal to, God and His eternal word, we are on a rocky and destructive path to nowhere.

The truth is we live in a promiscuous and rebellious world, where human beings want to do what feels good to them. Every man wants to behave in a way that seems "right in his own eyes.'" (Proverbs 21:2) And distressingly for the church, this attitude has crept into our ranks too.

The church that once laid down clear and strong guidelines for marriage, divorce and sexual behaviour in general began an unrighteous compromise without truly measuring the consequences. The more they compromised the more the people demanded and strangely this compromise did not make people satisfied and remain in the church, but caused them to leave in their masses.

Proverbs 22:28 warns us, "Do not remove the ancient landmark (or boundaries) which your fathers have set." How tempting to believe, in this enlightened and progressive age, that we can improve on the instructions of our ancient fathers or even readjust what our heavenly Father decrees and remove old, established and proven boundaries, without any backlash.

Every Christian leader knows it is never, never easy to say to the people in our care that certain behaviour is unacceptable and ungodly and unless they repent there will be both natural and spiritual consequences. I don't know of any church leader who enjoys saying, "that is sin and if you continue in it, appropriate action will have to be taken".

From time to time over the years, we have had to make such tough decisions about people's situations. We have shed tears with people wanting to get out of difficult and unhappy marriages, who have seen the possibility of happiness with someone else. We have wept with those whose sexual orientation was biblically prohibited. Do we enjoy making these decisions? You bet we don't. It is the part of leadership I hate the most, making decisions that affect people's lives and happiness. It's distressing, gives sleepless nights and a huge sense of inadequacy; nevertheless, leaders are called to lead.

The only thing that makes these decisions possible is to stand on, and even hide behind, God and His eternal and unchanging word. If He says it is right, it is right. If He says it is wrong, it is wrong and we forget and contradict this at our peril, as the Church of England is finding out. Such compromise will not strengthen any church (or indeed an individual) but weaken and deplete it. Unfortunately once this attitude is allowed to grip a church; it works like yeast, giving licence to others to behave similarly. And what we must never forget is that these God-given boundaries are not to inhibit and harm us, but for our protection and ultimate wellbeing.

And of course, not only the Church of England compromises. An Evangelical church in our city allowed two couples to change partners and re-married them. Another church overlooked their worship leader living with his girlfriend. And we all know and are bewildered by ministers who divorce and remarry, without biblical grounds, and yet somehow remain in leadership, confusing and distressing us all and making our jobs that much harder.

God forbid that we become judgmental, God help us to temper all our decisions with mercy, but let us be clear what God says in His word. Over and over again God's word says that sex before marriage, adultery, homosexuality and divorce and remarriage without biblical grounds, is sin and brings consequences. We cannot enforce these laws, cannot stop anyone committing sin, but we should and must warn them and as an absolute minimum, remove them from positions of ministry and leadership, both to discipline them and to protect the people. Pray for the Church of England. We are all needed to touch this great nation. Christianity in the west has been weakened by unrighteous compromise.

Chapter 15
Are We Becoming
A Marginalised Majority?

Please will someone, somewhere speak up. Speak up and remind Britain, its politicians and lawmakers, the PC (Politically Correct) lobby and the other faiths, that Great Britain is a Christian country. Our national churches are the Church of England, with our Christian Queen as its head, and the churches of Scotland, Wales and Ireland, all Christian churches, and yet more and more, like many of you, I feel part of a persecuted, misunderstood majority.

What has caused me this outbreak of pain? The latest incident was the sacking of a black, Christian therapist who refused to give sex education to a homosexual couple. A decent young man, forced by our laws, to choose between his God and the Bible and the prejudiced laws of our nation. In this case prejudiced, not against homosexuals, differing races, immigrants or other faiths, but against the Christian church.

And this is only the most recent act of discrimination, it seems every time I open a newspaper or watch the news, yet another Christian is on trial for their faith and for seeking to live by Gods standards. How much are we willing to take and remain passive?

We constantly read about people sacked or disciplined for wanting to wear a small, discreet cross as a symbol of their faith. While other faiths are allowed to wear different dress, often against company rules and also wear religious jewelry. I understand if, in some professions, jewelry is banned, but ban all jewelry, don't enforce it for the Christian and relax it for the people of other faiths. If a dress code of any type is operated, do it on a level playing field or as the famous quote goes, are some people really more equal than others.

Equally distressing are the Christian couple running a B & B in their own home, taken to court for refusing to allow a homosexual couple to share a bed. Thank God, common sense prevailed, but in our financially depressed nation, what a waste of taxpayers money. Yet just last week an apparently legal, "male homosexuals only" B & B was featured on a lifestyle programme on channel 4. If this is indeed legal practice, is the answer for Christians to advertise a B & B for married, heterosexuals only?

And just yesterday I read that a young, apparently mild-mannered, street preacher, after being questioned on the subject, was arrested for saying homosexuality was a sin. But listen to this, a renowned gay activist said that this action was ludicrous and that Christians should be allowed the freedom of speech to say what they believe just like everyone else! A wonderful part of the British heritage is freedom of speech, through the media we understand many abuse this privilege without penalty, but apparently, this freedom does not apply to the Christian. We are indeed a marginalised people.

And this is only the tip of the prejudice iceberg. Locally it filters through to churches struggling to get grants, to get planning permission to expand and other equal rights.

In the home, it's worrying about what our children will be taught, by law, in their state schools. It's worrying what they will be offered outside the home. Just recently a 13-year-old girl was given condoms in a park, by a youth worker, under the pretext of sex education.

Discrimination in all its forms is wrong. It is not right, it is not godly, but that also includes discrimination against the Christian majority (both committed and nominal) in Great Britain.

Our faith is not simply to believe and trust in Jesus Christ but to seek to obey and live by His word, as other faiths will understand. But we are being forced to choose between our faith in God and our nation.

Because we are so passive and accepting, the prejudice against us will not only continue but also increase. Let's remind ourselves that when faced by moneychangers in the temple, Jesus didn't stand by disapproving saying He'd pray about it. Prayer we know has tremendous power, but He was pro-active, made a whip and drove them out of the temple grounds. Surely the time has come to, metaphorically speaking, make a whip.

I, by no means and under no circumstances, advocate physical violence but if we don't stand together encourage and release strong, wise, outspoken leaders and resist this growing trend, who knows what the next generation will face.

The world has changed drastically in my lifetime. Many activities that are now legal and the right to practice them fiercely defended were once criminal. If in the last 50 years such massive change has occurred, and not always for the better, what might the next half-century bring in attitudes?

As in communist Russia in the 1950s, is it possible we won't be allowed to work because of our faith? Is there a chance our children will be removed from Christian homes? Will we be imprisoned for marrying? Will police be at the church doors listening to what we preach?

Denominational leaders, Bishops and Archbishops, Christian politicians and lawmakers, we, the people, the committed Christians in the churches across our land, implore you, -enough of apathy, lead us in speaking up for the Christian faith and lifestyle and demand to be heard. Let us not forget, it is these Christian values and standards that have made Britain so great, not just in Europe but in the world.

SECTION 3

Family

Chapter 16
Children

In our changing society, I believe that the biggest and most ferocious attack has been on Family and Marriage. The Spirit-Filled Life Bible says, "Family is the key component to society." There is an assault on that God ordained component, and society is disintegrating because of this. Marriage is disrespected and the vast majority of couples now co-habit at least for a period. We no longer refer to our husband or wife but our partners and in fact to ask about a persons husband or wife is now considered politically incorrect. The womb is now the most dangerous place for a child because of the increase in abortion. More than 50% of children are born outside marriage and in some cities, that number is more like 60%. Generations of young men are growing up without a stable father figure in their lives, therefore lacking a male role model and male discipline, hence the violence and criminality of our young men. 70% of young men in young offender institutions have no father in their lives.

When I consider these statistics, I want to lay my head in my hands and cry for our nation and for the generations of children we are failing. God forgive us, bring us to our knees in repentance, turn our nation around and cause us again to live by His God-given standards.

When I married David, I was just 19 years old. Perhaps because of my youth or perhaps because of "old wives tales", I was afraid of childbirth and married David on the understanding that we had no children. But Mother Nature is a very strong character and it was only a few years before I began to long for a child and didn't care too much what I had to endure to get one! I also reasoned that women all over the world went through this, not just once but many, many times, it therefore couldn't be too bad and it wasn't. I thank God with all my heart that my births were straightforward. The hospital staff and the comradeship with the other mothers afterwards were also wonderful. What I hadn't really understood or prepared for was the strength of my love for my children. But also the huge responsibility I felt for caring for these little human beings that God had entrusted to mine and David's care.

But I want to admit that this huge love was not consistent and the weight of responsibility sometimes upset and troubled me and I even occasionally wished I had waited a little longer before becoming a mother. But as my children flourished and grew, my apprehension eased and both David and I have thoroughly enjoyed being parents. But as I have said, it is a huge privilege and responsibility and needs to be taken seriously. It is a God-given task. Do you remember the story of Pharaoh's daughter finding Moses in the bulrushes? As she unwittingly handed him to his birth mother she said, "Raise this child for me and I will reward you." Exodus 2:8 When we become parents, whether by birth, fostering or adoption, this I believe is our commission from God, to raise this child for Him and He will reward us.

There are three basic responsibilities for we parents to work on. The first is that we should love our children (Titus 2:4). And although this seems obvious the problems sometimes lie in knowing how to express this love. We love our children by providing for them, feeding them, cleaning them and establishing a safe environment for them to grow in. But we also express this love by encouragement, affirmation and by giving them our time and attention. An ignored child is often a naughty child, as they seek our attention, even if that attention is negative. Many of us have to learn how to use our voice tone and facial expression to express love, a smile, putting feeling into our voice as we say, "Well done that's beautiful."

I am also a great believer in kisses and cuddles. Kiss, cuddle, stroke and hug your children as appropriate, all human beings need physical contact and if they don't receive parental love of this nature they will often look elsewhere while they are really still too young.

The second of our duties is to discipline our children, Proverbs 29:15 and 17. Love does not give children their own way. An undisciplined child is an unhappy child. Where our children won't listen to us and obey, some type of discipline will be necessary. I am from a generation who smacked their children occasionally but there are many other forms of appropriate discipline, time out, the naughty step, withdrawal of privileges etc., although I personally feel constant shouting, angry faces, verbal abuse, wrong expectations, intimidation etc. are damaging and destructive to any child. Let me just say two things though. Firstly, discipline your children while they are young, two to four years is an important phase. Once you have worked out the authority structure in your home, life is so much easier and calmer. Leave it till later and you will have a real struggle. They need to understand, very early, who are the parents and who are the children.

Secondly, don't antagonise your child, don't ask for a battle, avoid them if you can. E.g. warn them of impending bedtime so they can finish their game. How would you like to be scooped up in the middle of something interesting and carted off to bed! Ephesians 6:4 in the Good News Bible says, "Parents do not treat your children in such a way as to make them angry. Instead, bring them up with Christian discipline and instruction."

Training is our third responsibility. (Proverbs 22:6) We do this by letting them watch us or by showing them how to do things and letting them try. But we also train our children most importantly, by our example. I always remember a girlfriend being upset and angry with her little daughter's cheeky attitude. And one day I witnessed a confrontation between them. Mummy stuck her neck out, put her face in the little girls and shouted at her. In response, the little girl stuck her neck out, put her face in her mothers and shouted back! And it is possible to trace our children copying us in so many things. They pick up our mannerisms and language; they pick up our manners, our likes and dislikes. And when we are being a good example, it is hoped they pick up our beliefs also. But beware; they will also copy our bad examples. If we only go to church when it's convenient don't be surprised if as they grow older, church isn't important to them either.

Parents, our children are our God-given responsibility. In 1 Samuel 3:13, we read of Eli the priest who rose to the top of his profession but failed as a father. Consequently, he and his children all died prematurely.

I do not understand how people raise their children without God. But for we who know Him, His wisdom is available in every situation. And understand this early on, we all make mistakes; there isn't such a thing as a perfect parent. You do not know how many times I have had to ask God and my children to forgive me for not getting it right.

Chapter 17
Worth Fighting For Part 1

We all know, don't we, that Satan is a thief and a liar. If you couple this with the fact that many of we English find it hard to be assertive, let alone aggressive, the enemy gets away with far too much. But I want to remind us all that there are some things definitely worth fighting for. Our health matters, our marriages, our churches, the City where God has placed us and many other things in our lives, matter, but I particularly want to talk about fighting for our children.

David and I have two sons, Jason and Jarrod, conceived and raised for God and could not be more loved, precious and important in our lives, as most children are. I don't want to shock you, but for us certainly having greater priority than any ministry!

There have been times in their lives when we have had to fight alongside them or for them. On one major occasion, they were in their mid-teens and going through that period many young people go through, when they ask, "Is the God of my parents, my God too?" Jason, who was about sixteen years old at the time, says he loved God, but was finding the church difficult and couldn't identify with his Christian peers. He was also hurt on our behalf at occasional criticism and problems within the church. He came on Sunday mornings because he knew this was our desire and because his love and respect for us had never altered, for which we thank him and God.

Jarrod, about 14 years at this point, was in church regularly and in fact already in the worship group, but outside of his music, totally spiritually introverted and unable to verbalise or express his feelings towards or about God. At one point he was put out of the worship group for not being a worshipper! That's given us a few laughs since, considering his present ministry.

Things came to a head in a mid-week meeting with a guest speaker from the U.K., Paul Newberry. At the end of the meeting, he called forward all youth for prayer. Because it was mid-week Jason wasn't in the meeting and Jarrod, who had been on the keyboard, ran out of the church as if Satan himself was after him. I looked at the shiny, happy faces of our church youth waiting for prayer, from all sorts of different backgrounds and although I was thrilled at their openness to the Spirit, my own children, raised for God, were not there. Deeply distressed, I ran out to the little kitchen at the back of the hall and began to cry. Not polite little sniffles, but great racking, noisy sobs. Some of the women came out to see what was wrong and all I could say was "My children, my children!" The enemy told me I was one lousy mother and a lousy Christian too since I had been unable to influence even my children for Jesus. (Remember he is a thief and a liar.)

Something broke in me that day and a new assertiveness even aggression grew in me. Satan was not having my sons. I submitted to God, I asked him to forgive any parenting mistakes I may have made; (children don't come with a manual, do they?) And in spite of my love for the boys, I genuinely didn't know if I always got it right. I asked Him to guide me as a parent at this point in their lives, when to speak, what to say, when to keep silent.

And I resisted the enemy. David and I began to pray with renewed determination and faith for a spiritual breakthrough for our sons. I spoke in tongues as I cleaned their room; I laid my hand on their empty beds and claimed them for God. When our children are small, we can accompany them almost everywhere, but who knows teenage boys are not too keen to have Mum or Dad tag along with them socially! So whenever they left the house, we asked God to appoint angels to keep them, protect them, to allow them to do nothing that would damage their lives.

I would like to tell you this battle lasted a few weeks and we saw a breakthrough, but that wouldn't be true. It happened gradually over a period of several years and involved the input of many other men and women of God. Some battles are not quick ones unfortunately. But God was faithful and by nineteen years of age Jarrod was actually in ministry, having had a tremendous breakthrough spiritually and it's almost impossible now to believe he was ever inhibited!

Jason took a little longer but gradually, after we returned to Britain, he began to meet Christians, through his career, that he respected and liked and with whom he could identify. He worked at that time in outdoor education and has since moved on to management training. After working for 2 years with Christian Aid agencies in both Afghanistan and Kosovo during the troubles and seeing God do tremendous things for him, he returned to the Lake District where he first attended a live Anglican church. Now he is in a live charismatic church in the area, and is a wonderful, natural evangelist.

Do you remember Shammah who stood in the field of lentils and decided, "So far enemy but no further" and by God's help protected the crop? (2 Samuel 23:11-12) God give us this attitude when the enemy seeks to steal and destroy what God has given or entrusted to us.

When we feel overwhelmed, weak, outnumbered or defenceless, remember how Elisha prayed for his servant, "Open his eyes Lord, that he may see how many angels fight on our behalf." 2 Kings 6:17

People who know me, know I dislike ornaments, but in spite of this, in my home is a small, cheap, brass plaque, we have had it almost as long as we have been married. It has travelled back and fore across Europe with us, when far more precious and expensive items were left behind. It is because on this plaque is a declaration David and I made very early on in our relationship, "As for me and my house, we will serve the Lord." Joshua 24:15

David and I made that promise for ourselves, for our children and even for our grandchildren, as yet unborn; Satan certainly isn't robbing us of household salvation without resistance. Mothers, Fathers, stand in your home and declare, "Satan - no further, this is God's territory." And remember that although our enemy is undoubtedly strong and wily our God is even stronger and it is He and His angels who fight with us for our children.

Chapter 18
Worth Fighting For
Part 2

Of all the articles I have written for "Joy", none has brought more response from you than the article on "Fighting for your Children". E-mails, phone calls and letters tell me how important your children are to you too. Whether they are 3 months, 3 years or 30 years old, the vast majority of us would give our lives for our children, no matter how old they are, they are still "our babies". We would give almost anything to protect them from pain, disappointment, discouragement or any other negative. Yet our sensible side knows that not only is that impossible, it would be downright unhealthy. We cannot protect them from every ill, they have to mature, stand on their own feet and know that only God will always be there for them as their support and protection.

I want to tell you two very different stories of how I would have done anything to spare my sons their pain. David and I walked these troubled paths with them, but ultimately they know it was God who brought them through and the experiences matured and strengthened them spiritually.

When Jason was 13 years old and at school in Gibraltar, he experienced a season of bullying. It was a distressing and worrying time for us all. He had, he confessed, made a negative comment about another boy's football skills. Lesson one, be more diplomatic! After school, about 50 boys gathered around him, shouting, threatening and trying to force a fight between the two. Jay was not harmed physically in any way, but the psychological effect on him was temporarily devastating. Continuing intimidation, negative comments and animosity, compounded the incident in his mind. He became depressed, fearful and began what the doctor described as pediatric vomiting.

It was upsetting to see him in this state. Our kids spend so much time in school, don't they, that such bullying affects a huge part of their lives. He had flatly refused to be accompanied to and from school, when much of the intimidation took place, feeling this would exacerbate the problem. So we decided to defend our son from this physical and emotional attack, spiritually.

Every morning we read protection scriptures over his life. He needed to know that Mum and Dad couldn't always be with him and as the years roll on, it simply isn't appropriate, but God could and would. We prayed for him, speaking peace, rebuking the fear and spirit of intimidation and praying for the other boys. Then we all synchronised our watches and wherever we were, it was our agreement, our pact that 5 minutes before class ended, we would begin to pray God's peace, protection and wisdom over him, until he walked safely through our door. I remember part way through our battle, Jay said in a poignant little voice, "Mum, whatever God is trying to teach me, I hope I hurry up and learn it." Gradually his fears subsided, the incident faded and the boys resumed an easier relationship.

Understand, I'm not saying don't go down all the normal, natural routes to end bullying for your child, visit the school, do everything necessary, but bring God naturally and powerfully right to the point of your child's need. At 3 we can accompany them everywhere, at 30 we can't; only God can do that.

Jason has since been in many dangerous and frightening situations and had to face great animosity. He spent a year in Afghanistan and a year in Kosovo at the time of their troubles, as an Aid Worker. His experiences as a 13-year-old boy taught him, "With my God, I am safe,"

The second incident involved Jarrod. He was about 26 years old and travelling extensively in ministry. This particular year, he had spent 3 months, in two separate stretches, in Africa. For this extended period, he had been taking a very powerful anti-malarial drug.

As he flew home at the end of his second trip, he felt God tell him, he would enter a wilderness experience. As he returned home, he was back living with us for a period, having left Bible School; he said he felt unwell with flu-like symptoms. He took to his bed or the settee and over the next few days, the symptoms grew. He became extremely fearful, unwilling to go out or be left alone. He awoke at night with panic attacks. (He countered this by playing Psalms quietly on a C.D., so as he awoke, God's word was the first thing he heard.) He became hypochondriac. Every spot, lump, or strange feeling was cause for fear. Our confident, gifted, anointed, happy, well-travelled son appeared almost broken. We have never cried so much in our home as we did at that time. It was very frightening. What was happening to him? Was he on the verge of a breakdown? What had caused this?

Fortunately, on a T.V. consumer programme, the anti-malarial drug was coming under scrutiny, although excellent protection, for some people it had huge side effects. Many people studied, had similar symptoms to Jarrod. A T.V. cameraman, who had travelled the world, was now unable to work. Some had even committed suicide, although it was hard to prove the drug was the only cause.

Jarrod visited the doctor a couple of times but wasn't really taken too seriously. The third time an old locum was in the surgery and this time David accompanied him saying, "Please listen to my son, this is completely out of character". The old doctor listened long and hard, took time to examine him carefully and then to explain, it was a form of depression and yes, perhaps caused by the anti-malarial drug. He offered anti-depressants which Jarrod refused saying, now he knew the cause, he would fight it.

Every trip out, every time he was left alone, called for a time of prayer, resisting, binding, declaring God's word. He would drive from the house blasting godly music to counter the panic and fear in his mind. We have a picture of him at this time when we visited his brother in the Lakes and although he is laughing, the fear is in his eyes.

Six weeks, 40 days of wilderness experience, after returning home from Africa, we were all at a 40th birthday party. I looked across the room to check he was alright, something I had started to do during this illness, and saw him laughing and talking normally. Whatever it was, it was broken. For 2 years the symptoms persisted in a much milder form, but God had brought him and us through.

"Sons are a heritage from the Lord, children a reward from Him... Blessed is the man whose quiver is full of them, they will not be put to shame when they contend with their enemies in the gate." (Psalm127) We had contended with our enemies and with our God, we had won.

Chapter 19
Marriage: The "F" Plan

It was March 21st, 1964 and 2.30pm. I was nineteen years old and it was my wedding day, and like so many other brides before and since, I was deeply in love. But unlike, - I believe the statistic is now 40% of brides, - 43 years later I am still married, yes, to the same man and happy. (As I put these articles into a book, it is 2017 and we have been married for 53 years!)

If only we knew why some marriages last and others don't, perhaps the western trend for broken promises could be halted.

Here is my F-Plan (remember the diet) for a long-lasting and happy marriage.

Fancy

You have to fancy each other, and although love in our society has wrongly come to mean sex, lust and romance, I believe you still have to desire each other physically. When you are young this is so easy, spontaneous and enjoyable, but as we reach middle age it's something that has to be worked at. Mental and physical weariness, responsibilities and so many other changes call for thought and determination to keep this side fresh and alive. Instead of falling into bed at 11.30pm after a hectic day, and still enjoying each other, now we have to make a date. Once we took our looks for granted; now we have to work at our attractiveness.

Faithfulness

This is going to sound so old-fashioned, but this is how David and I have lived and protected our marriage. Faithfulness for us is far more than abstaining from intimate physical contact with the opposite sex. Faithfulness for us has been a matter of heart, mind and spirit faithfulness. We are each other's closest friend and confidant and although we have other friends, we don't share with others what we don't share with each other.

We don't counsel or spend time alone with members of the opposite sex, - we protect our marriage. Loyalty is also important. We don't expose our spouse's weaknesses outside of the marriage, not even to family. I once had a friend who constantly criticised her husband and children. What does Proverbs say? - "The wisest of women builds her house, but folly with her own hands tears it down." (Proverbs 14:1) - And that is exactly what happened, her family disintegrated.

Thirdly Faults and Failings

Don't look for them, because you will find them. Although on my wedding day I was so in love, I have to confess I haven't woken every morning since, looked at the face on the pillow beside me and thought "How blessed I am!" And although David is too gallant to admit it, I'm sure he has felt the same. A ploy of our enemy (who, remember, hates marriage, hence the state of the world,) is to magnify and concentrate our thoughts on our spouse's faults. But what does Peter say? "Above all, keep loving one another earnestly, since love covers a multitude of sins." (1Peter 4:8) When I am feeling less than enamored of my husband, I remember his positive points and what he has added and continues to add to my life.

Forgiveness

It's another good F-word when we do fail each other. One year David gave me a Valentine greeting on his computer, - that took forgiveness!

Faith

Fifthly, is our shared Faith. This for us is the cement that holds us together. When we were so young that we barely knew what we were saying, we made vows before a God who did. When things are hard, prayer changes things. God is for marriage! And don't ask God to change your spouse, but to change you. "Lord, I want to love him, I want a successful, loving, respectful, passionate marriage. I don't want to endure it just because I made vows, I want to enjoy it." Ecclesiastes 4:12 says a threefold cord is not easily broken. Jesus is the third cord. In our wedding, as our first act after taking our vows, we took communion. It symbolically declared, "Lord, you are First."

Fun

Then there's Fun. Life is for laughing and too many marriages end or are simply endured because the fun, the laughter, the shared pleasures are neglected. Many years ago in the church we belonged to, a young couple were pressurized into marriage because a very short relationship had produced a pregnancy.

For the first year or so, it was evident that the young man and woman were deeply unhappy. Animosity hung in the air and red eyes were evidence of private anguish. But then gradually they began to change and seemed much happier. I plucked up the courage to ask what had happened. The reply was "We realized we laughed at the same things," Humour kept them together and they are still together more than thirty years later.

You don't have to spend much to have fun. Go out for coffee, walk hand in hand along a beach. Take a weekend break in a lovely hotel. Laugh at life, laugh at yourself, laugh with each other. We are going to have lines as we get older, that's for certain, - at least let them be laughter lines.

My F Plan has simplified things a bit and there are other important factors, which I can't find an "F" for. Things like mutual respect, affirming each other, manners are very important, as is communication and so is something I can only describe as "bonding". We are a unit, a whole, hurt him and you hurt me, don't say one word of criticism about him because I won't listen. His successes are my successes and his failures my failures. Just as Genesis says – "We are one."

Now, so many years after first writing this article, I want to add a couple of other F words! David and I had never dreamt that marriage in our senior years could still be difficult and perhaps the truth is that we will never stop working at our marriages! Someone keeps moving the goalposts!

Foibles

The first new F-word is 'foibles'! We all seem to develop them to a lesser or greater extent as we grow older, little habits and rituals that punctuate our days. Such things as falling asleep in front of the TV! And one of the things we need to work at is accepting each other's little foibles.

Forbearance

And the last F-word is Forbearance. With increasing years comes just a little less energy, a little less vitality, a little less drive. I never thought this would happen but I find myself married to an old man! But here is an even more staggering fact; my husband is married to a 'more than mature' woman! At this stage forbearing with one another in love is incredibly important. Yet, old or not, we thank God from the bottom of our hearts that we still have each other.

See also Chapter 28, Submission in Marriage.

Chapter 20
Attitudes To Sex
Part 1: To Wait Is Best

I was alone in my favourite coffee shop the other day, reading a newspaper. So often at times like this, I'm distressed and annoyed by what I read. It could be my advancing years, but so often now, I don't understand the mentality of so many people.

This was an article about promiscuity in the mid-teens, of one-night stands and multiple partners, of venereal disease accepted as an option, of the aggressive predatory sexuality of the young girl as well as the young boy, of sex without love or responsibility.

How times have changed! If you're a younger person reading this, I don't mean sex, sex has been around for a long time, your generation didn't invent it. But our fundamental attitude to it has changed. I don't even mean that my generation or my parents' generation didn't have sex before marriage, because of course many did, but it was considered wrong, the forbidden fruit. One kept it a secret, even the unsaved girls I worked with in the bank would have been deeply offended if someone had even suggested they "went too far" as we called it. An affair within the staff in the bank led to shock and disgust and an official investigation.

How different today where sex is expected early in a relationship with no commitment attached. Sexual exploits are a subject for bragging and comparison. Adultery no longer raises an eyebrow, where "no holds are barred".

I deeply regret this decline, where everywhere this new standard is forced upon us. Even the most apparently harmless 'soap', on early enough for the youngest child to see, at least implies sex outside marriage takes place, sometimes between schoolchildren, sometimes even same sex.

My husband occasionally treats me to a women's magazine and I've had to ask him to check the contents. What was once the domain of fashion, home, cookery and helpful tips has become the world of sordid stories and graphic sexual advice. If I had a young daughter, I would certainly be checking the contents of her reading material, where early sexuality is encouraged in teen magazines simply by being mentioned at all.

Our Christian youngsters are under such pressure to conform, where to "go too far" is considered the norm and right, but to stay pure and chaste is considered "weird and abnormal". What does the Bible say "where righteousness is called sin, and sin righteousness" (Isaiah 5.20)

One of our young girls was telling me that her workmates took it for granted that she was sleeping with her boyfriend and she was criticised, ridiculed and her sexuality brought into question when she said she wasn't.

And make no mistake about it, the Bible says this promiscuity damages, but experience also confirms this. I was watching a programme that touched on prostitution in America and the "Madam" was saying that the girls needed regular time out. Why? Because she says, every encounter took something from them, depleted them emotionally, the Bible would say spiritually too. The act of sex is not simply the conjoining of two bodies, but there is a spiritual and emotional significance also. (1Corinthians 6:15-20)

Somehow we have to reinforce in our young people to be pure and proud of it. That to wait is best. That there is no greater joy and no greater turn on than knowing on your wedding night, that this is the first time, that you have saved yourself for each other. There is no greater blessing for your future marriage than knowing you did it

God's way.

We visited a Christian school recently where many of the young girls wore a silver ring as a reminder of a promise that they would wait for sex until marriage. God bless them for understanding that "No" is a good answer, that abstinence before marriage is a virtue. They are wise to understand that purity would stem the Aids epidemic and the venereal disease onslaught, that chastity is the best birth control of all. Medical knowledge tells us that sex too early in life, especially for young women, is damaging for their future health. God bless these young people and strengthen them in their resolve.

The world, through the media, forces free sex at us constantly. We need to counteract this by talking freely and openly about the joy of waiting and doing it God's way.

Chapter 21
Attitudes To Sex
Part 2: Bible Blessed Sex

Lest anyone should think from the last chapter that I, or more importantly God and the Bible, are in any way anti-sex, I thought I'd better follow it up, because of course, nothing could be further from the truth. Sex is God's idea and God's plan. Right in the beginning when God made Adam and then gave him a "help meet" in Eve, He instructed them "Go multiply and be fruitful", Genesis 1:28, which of course involves the act of sex.

Here is a riddle. What is a sin and forbidden by God one day, but the next day is a virtue, blessed and encouraged by the Almighty? - The act of sex, of course. The night before your marriage it continues to be a sin, but once married God says go for it!

And there is nothing stuffy or prim and proper about God in this either. Proverbs tells us "Live happily with the wife of your youth and may her breasts ever satisfy you, may you ever be captivated by her love." Proverbs 5:15-20

Song of Solomon is God's book on marital love, even glancing through, this is obvious but better teachers than I, tell us this is a book of erotica, sexual love between a man and his lover wife, and when fully understood apparently quite detailed.

Hebrews 13:4 tells us "Marriage is honourable and the bed

undefiled." There is nothing to feel shame or embarrassment about in any way, once you are married; on the sexual front its all systems go.

But sometimes the attitude of the world taints and spoils the purity of sex in Christian marriage.

Many years ago, when we were newly married, another young couple that married about the same time, had real sexual problems. Brought up in Christian homes, the young woman had picked up the attitude from her parents and grandparents that sex was dirty, sinful, just for having babies, obviously something we Christian parents need to guard against when teaching our children. I remember our pastor's advice to this day. He instructed them to make love on Sunday mornings before coming to church, as a spiritual act of service to each other before God! In the days of up to 5 meetings on a Sunday, my attitude might have been, "Oh one more thing to do on Sundays then!"

Some years after this, David and I were involved with a young Christian couple near where we lived, who had terrible sexual hang-ups. They had sex before marriage and somehow, in spite of repentance, couldn't release themselves from this guilt, (because of course, God had forgiven them.) Each time they did make love, which was rarely anyway and only when the temptation became too much, the husband made them both "repent" afterwards. We were quite young ourselves and actually had to call in a church elder to help, but this false guilt wasn't broken and they eventually split up.

How the enemy can destroy us in this area. If he cannot persuade us to have sex with anything or anyone, he persuades us that sex even with our life partner is wrong. Let's remember that Satan is a thief and a liar. If as Christians he cannot persuade us into promiscuity, he seeks to persuade us that sex per se is wrong and steal from us, as married couples, a God-given gift.

Even Paul, strict as he was, strait-laced as he appears, tells us not to defraud each other physically, to have sex regularly to keep temptation away. To withhold sex only by mutual agreement for prayer and fasting and then not to do it for too long. 1 Corinthians 7:5

Sex through our married lives can be many things. It can be experimental, passionate, loving, intimate, to produce children, fun, funny, comforting, physically releasing, affirming etc. On our wedding night a huge adventure with our spouse begins and through the years it grows and changes, by the time you reach our age, you are just incredibly grateful that you can still do it! But know this, no matter what our age, God has given us sex as a precious, special gift from Him, and as with all His gifts, it is important that we use it, develop it, practice it, make time for it and probably most of all enjoy it!

Chapter 22
Christmas Memories

As I look back down the years of my many Christmases, if I am truthful, only a few really stand out as unforgettable and precious. My childhood Christmases have almost all rolled into one warm memory of my family, many who have now died, a pillowcase of small gifts, an open fire, oranges and nuts. But as I grew older several stand out in my mind as strong, precious and individual memories. Christmas 1962 I met my husband at a Christian Christmas house party in Bryn Eirias Hall, Colwyn Bay. I was there with the youth from my church in Strelley, Nottingham and David was there with his parents. His 14-year-old sister, who had downs syndrome, had died that year and the family couldn't face Christmas at home without her. Memories of someone we have loved deeply but have lost, perhaps to death, can be particularly painful at this time of year. But Patti's death brought David and I together. Boxing evening David drove me to Llandudno and we sat and watched the snowfall over the bay. It was very romantic and that Christmas changed and set the course for my life.

A few years later, it was our first baby's second Christmas, he was 16 months old. We had bought him, second hand, a large furry dog on wheels, big enough to sit on but also a push-along toy. He tore off the paper and was so thrilled with it; he ate his breakfast with one arm around the dog's neck, how easy it was to please him!

Christmas 1978 was our families first year in Gibraltar and we realised our children had made huge sacrifices because of our calling.

So we decided to give them an extra special gift to say thank you. So on this Christmas, the boys had opened all their usual presents of books, games, chocolates etc. and then David said, "Oh we've forgotten something." He went into our bedroom and returned with a large box. The boys excitedly tore off the wrapping and yelled with delight at a Scalextric set, (electric cars that race around a track, the in-toy at that time.) It was a huge surprise and treat for them, they played with it for hours, both stretched out on the carpet and enjoyed it so much.

The only problem is, ever since that time, I want to recreate those Christmas memories every year. I want to see that same joy and excitement as our sons open their gifts, even though they are now men. They tell me I'm being unreasonable and my expectations are too high. They say to get that reaction now, we'd have to gift wrap a sports car or a Harley Davidson!

But isn't it true that one of the lovely things about this time of year, is giving presents to those we love and seeing their pleasure and appreciation? When we have taken time and effort to choose and wrap gifts, it is important to get a positive reaction. I like to give gifts that will surprise or amuse or that will simply be used regularly.

If we feel this way, how does God the Father feel when He has given the most costly gift He could ever give, His only precious Son, to have so much of mankind reject Him? To hear so many say "No thanks, I don't need Him or want Him, return to sender." Have you ever been to M&S straight after Christmas and seen the huge queues returning unwanted or not quite appropriate gifts? How must the Father feel when we treat His precious gift like an M&S wrong size, wrong colour sweater, returned, unwanted, unopened and unappreciated?

We are amused when small children often unwrap their gifts but then proceed to play with the paper, the box and the string and leave the real gift in a corner untouched! But how sad and tragic that this is also, so often, the world's reaction when they amuse themselves at Christmas with the baby in a manger, the star, the shepherds and the wise men, traditional Christmas wrapping paper, but leave the real gift unrecognised, unused and discarded, they simply wanted a religious Christmas.

We live in a materialistic, wealthy world where it is harder and harder to find gifts that will thrill and delight people who have everything already. But as we approach another festive season, let's count as secondary these materialistic commercial trappings the world has persuaded us we need and concentrate on the most precious, most exciting, most beautiful, most useful and needed gift we could ever receive from a Father with a heart of love, who understands us better than we understand ourselves. Don't let's forget to thank Him. To kiss Him in worship and to recognise the importance of taking pleasure in His gift, not just once in a while but for every moment of our lives.

"This is how much God loved the world: He gave His Son, His one and only Son. And this is why: so that no one need be destroyed; by believing in Him, anyone can have a whole and lasting life." John 3:16 (The Message)

Chapter 23
Keep Christ In Christmas

After all these years of writing for JOY, I have a dreadful and embarrassing confession to make. I hate Christmas. I sometimes feel I'm the only Christian in the whole world that dislikes this season. I don't like winter when the celebrating occurs, I don't even like Christmas food; brussel sprouts and roast parsnips will be my favourites on Christmas day. What a scrooge I am!

But when I stop and think about it, it isn't so much the occasion I dislike, as what we in the 21st-century western world, have done to it.

On one hand, we have commercialised it beyond recognition. This year, even earlier than usual, at the end of August, when we are still wearing linen and our legs are still bare and brown, the shops, in a desperate attempt to increase profits in such a difficult year, began to display Christmas fare. Four whole months of glitter, cards and wrapping paper for just a one or two-day celebration! Clothes too are all red, black, silver and gold as if we all spend winter partying. I don't want this to sound like sour grapes, but in my life, I for one, need very few party outfits. Each year media pressure escalates to pressurise parents to go to great lengths to acquire, for their much-loved children, this year's favourite toy. And especially in this year of extreme financial problems, in a well-intentioned effort not to disappoint, thousands of us will go into debt, paying for Christmas well into summer, to provide all the material trappings we consider essential to a good Christmas time.

Add to this, disturbingly and distressingly, November, December and January are "no go" areas in many of our cities because of drunkenness and alcohol abuse, our world's idea of celebrating, it is not the most peaceful of seasons. And the most sensible of us, including me, spend December shopping and cooking for a two-day festival and then spend January dieting.

Selflessness, love and reconciliation turned into a festival of materialism, drunkenness and gluttony. On the other hand, the world seeks to take Christ completely and entirely out of Christmas. I read last year that only one in five primary schools will have a nativity play and the others will replace it with pantomimes such as Hansel and Gretel. Our church parents also tell me that many advent calendars now go up to New Year, therefore celebrating the advent of the year and not the advent of Jesus Christ. It has also become increasingly difficult to find faith cards to send, Santa and the robin have well and truly replaced Jesus.

Our politically correct nation cancels the Christ of Christmas to avoid offence to other faiths and the secular. But our family has lived and worked with Muslims, Jews and Indians of several faiths. We have attended their marriages and even some of their festivals and I want to categorically say, they are not offended by our faith in Jesus Christ, they are offended by our lack of faith, morals and ethics, this they do not like or understand.

For a few years, I have been on a serious but good-natured campaign to keep Christ in Christmas. I don't mind Santa Claus, but please don't give him special powers, don't make him all seeing, all knowing and overly generous. I don't mind the tree, the baubles, crackers, turkey etc. but let us remember what they are, Christmas trimmings, central is the Christ child, without Him it's just another winter's day. I never write Xmas, no matter how busy or flustered, X signifies unknown. I make every attempt to buy faith cards and always write something spiritual even if it's only "God bless you this Christmas", even to my neighbours, in a feeble attempt to bring God into the season again.

Because this is what Christmas is all about, Almighty God, creator of heaven and earth, out of love for us, becoming a human baby, entrusted to the womb and arms of a young virgin girl. In all that we do this Christmas, may we Christians never forget this. I know there is a sense in which we remember this every day, but it is also a wonderful time to remind our sceptical world. As you and your family celebrate the season, in whatever way your family enjoys, may the Christ of Christmas bring you His eternal gifts that cost us nothing, but cost Him His all. May His love, joy and peace, be in your hearts and in your homes.

Unto us, a child is born, Unto us, a son is given,

And the government will be on His shoulders.

And He will be called

Wonderful Counsellor,

Mighty God,

Everlasting Father, Prince of Peace.

Isaiah 9:6

Chapter 24
We Are A Grandmother

At last I can say, in the famous words of Margaret Thatcher, "We are a grandmother!" Zachary Benjamin was born safely on January 31st 2009. Mother and baby are both well and very beautiful.

I have prayed for this little boy and any other grandchildren I may eventually have, for many, many years, when even my own sons were still in their youth. I prayed not simply that he would be, because I never doubted that one day I would be a grandmother, even though it has been quite a long time in coming. But I prayed for him as a person, as a boy and eventually as a man. My prayer is that he will be healthy, strong and happy. That he will be prosperous, have self-esteem, strong relationships and be fulfilled in his life. But I don't only pray that he will succeed in his earthly life, but that he will become a man who knows and serves God. His father Jarrod, is the third generation Assemblies of God minister. My fervent prayer is that Zachary too, will serve our God, that he will make a difference in his time and generation, that he will see the hand of God move in our world in a greater and more powerful way than all the generations before him.

We must never be presumptuous or complacent that because generations in our family have served God, that this blessing is guaranteed to continue. It is our parental and grandparental responsibility to live in such a way that our offspring are drawn to the immortal God and His Son Jesus Christ. They need to see the joy, peace, power, integrity and blessing in our lives and come to understand not only that God is, but He is also "a rewarder of those who diligently seek Him".

Many years ago, when Jason was a tiny boy, he said to my mother-in-law, "Nana, you and Granddad love Jesus like we do, don't you?" He saw in his paternal grandparents a living faith to which, eventually, he also aspired. Paul in writing to Timothy refers to the faith, which he saw first in his grandmother Lois and then in his mother Eunice and which, now, Paul also sees clearly in Timothy. I am convinced that there is a connection in this statement.

But, and this is what we must see clearly, it is not automatic. Our responsibility to following generations must be taken seriously. The priest Eli was punished for not training and disciplining his sons correctly and sadly his children also suffered. In fact, 1 Samuel 2:12 says tragically, "The sons of Eli were corrupt, they did not know the Lord." He may have been a priest and therefore, hopefully, a man of God, but he was not a good father. We don't just bring children into the world to feed them, clothe them and educate them. Our greatest and most lasting responsibility is to sow the things of God into their tiny hearts, sharing our faith with them, increasing in maturity until they are grown. (Have you noticed, children often make several decisions for Jesus as they mature and their understanding increases. Each decision is powerful, legitimate and really important in their walk with God.)

The children of Israel also experienced spiritual decline in their families. After generations walking with God and experiencing over and over again miraculous deliverance, protection and provision, a generation arose who were half-hearted in their commitment. Joshua had to challenge them, "Who will you serve?" (Joshua 24:15) And although they chose God, it was, scripture shows us, a less than whole-hearted decision. The dreadful consequences are found in Judges 2:10 "Another generation arose after them who did not know the Lord."

One of the blessings as we grow older, for those who know the Lord, is to see our children's children, (Psalm 128:6) but this also brings responsibility to pray for and influence this next generation for God.

It is another chance to be wholehearted and sow the Kingdom into young hearts. And if your grandchildren are on the other side of the world or if for dreadful reasons of family breakdown, you rarely or never see them, remember there is always the power of prayer that knows no boundaries. Never give up praying for them.

I don't know of any Christian ancestors in my family yet miraculously aged eight years, I began to search for God and feel His call on my life. But I do remember that my much loved Grandma Hogg had a Bible by her bedside and is it too fanciful to wonder, when I reach heaven, will she or some other grandparent in my past step forward and assure me, "My granddaughter, I prayed for you."

SECTION 4

Spiritual Keys

I have found, in the Christian life, that there are keys that unlock the treasure troves of heaven. At first glance they are ordinary and insignificant and could easily be ignored or overlooked but used regularly they open doors to blessing, fullness, provision, relationship and so much more. As a young woman I worked for a high street Bank, and from time to time held one of the keys to the bank's strong room. The key looked ordinary and very much like the old-fashioned backdoor key to a house. In truth that key opened the door to the wealth of an international bank. So it is with these and many other "spiritual keys", they unlock the wealth of heaven and the kingdom, use them continuously.

Chapter 25
Time

I have apparently written this article for a Christmas edition of the magazine "Joy" but it is, in reality, an article about understanding the importance of "time" and "timing".

Doesn't time fly? I am writing this article in early October and for several weeks tinsel, cards and jolly Santas have been appearing in the shops, by my timing, just a little too early. Do you remember the children's game, "What time is it, Mr Wolf?" We played this game in a day and age before computer games and when children still had legs and lots of freedom! And as we reach yet another Christmas and finish another year, it is important to know "What time it is", in our individual lives.

I am a woman obsessed with time. I am never without a watch; even sunning myself on a Greek beach I need my watch. I don't trust my inner clock to tell me when it's time for coffee and lunch, and what a calamity if I should miss it!

Have you noticed too, that time, although so apparently rigid, moves at a different pace according to your age and situation? At my age, time speeds by and I cannot believe yet another year is almost gone. And yet all over the Christian world, children are wondering will Christmas ever arrive, as time moves so slowly for them.

Time, even at Christmas, remains the most precious thing we can give the people we love, our children, spouses, friends and even our

God.

Time is also a great healer, and in times of great pain we can encourage ourselves, "this too will pass".

The Bible also says time and indeed timing is important. One of the tribes of Israel, the tribe of Issachar, had this attribute, they understood the times and seasons, (1 Chronicles 12:32) when to act, when to wait.

Ecclesiastes 3:1-8, says there is a right time for everything. (How I wish our retail trade understood this concept.)

And in our spiritual life, to avoid disappointment and heartache, to achieve our potential, it is vital that we know as individuals "the time" in which we are living.

Let me give you some examples from the Bible of the understanding of time.

In Exodus, after the children of Israel were released from captivity and miraculously crossed the Red Sea, it took them 40 years to complete an 11-day journey into the promised land of Canaan. Fear and disobedience, lack of faith and courage, caused the Israelites to wander aimlessly in the desert until that generation of unbelievers died out. Put simply, the children of Israel WASTED TIME. Nevertheless, and amazingly, God's hand remained on them in guiding, protection and provision.

If we don't take care, we can wander around in a spiritual desert of unfulfilled promises and unreached potential. If we are filled with fear and lack courage, if we see our enemies as giants and ourselves as grasshoppers, we too will waste time.

Now the young man Joseph believed God and embraced the calling on his life but many years and many horrendous trials had to be endured before he fulfilled his destiny. (Genesis 37:50)

What was happening here? On this occasion, God was preparing and growing a young man to fulfil his calling. It was A TIME OF PREPARATION. In times of great problems, it is not the trial that is important, but how we react to it. Will it break us or will it make us stronger, the choice is ours?

To achieve our destiny in God, we must grow our character, become mature and whole in Him, and unfortunately, it is so often in the hard times that our growth occurs.

If this is where you are today, hold the dream, don't be disheartened, you are in a time of preparation.

The patriarch Abraham had been promised a son in his old age. But 20 years passed before the fulfilment of that promise. What was happening this time? Who can tell why God delayed; Abraham was simply in A TIME OF WAITING, probably the hardest time of all. But not understanding this and filled with impatience, Abraham fathered Ishmael (Genesis 16) and gave our world, even to this day, one of its greatest human problems. When we are in a time of waiting, we need to take care and remember Abraham's rashness and the pain and heartache this caused everyone. Let's declare, If God has said it, He will do it. Yes, He needs our co-operation, but He doesn't need our help or manipulation.

Finally, Esther was a young Jewish orphan, raised by her Uncle Mordecai. She was taken into the harem of the foreign King Xerxes because of her beauty and eventually chosen as his queen. Meanwhile, her Uncle uncovered a plot to destroy the Jews and he called on her to use her now privileged position to speak to the King and deliver her people. Forbidden to go into the King's presence unless invited, this was a dangerous mission. Her Uncle reminds her, she may well have come into this royal role for such a time as this. (Esther 4:14) She eventually accepts her calling, bravely declaring, "If I perish, I perish." There is no doubt Esther was in A TIME OF DESTINY.

The call of God is rarely convenient, easy or glamorous but there are times in our life when the call is definitely urgent. God may even have been stirring us for some time, then a day comes when we hear His voice, His calling, "Whom shall I send and who will go for us."

In our time of destiny, God grant us the courage to respond like Esther and Isaiah, "Here am I, send me." (Isaiah 6:8)

As we approach the changing of yet another year, do you have your spiritual watch on, what time is it in your life?

"But I trust in you O Lord,

I say, "You are my God,"

My times are in your hands." Psalm 31:15

"Trust also in Him and He will bring it to pass." Psalm 37:5

Chapter 26
Power In Worship

I want to share with you the most important key to successful Christian living that I have found in all my 60+ years walking with Jesus. It is so simple, so easy to do, costs very little, is incredibly enjoyable, is better than a facelift in my opinion and has amazing results. This key is worship. Yes I know we all know about it and have had mountains of teaching on it, but the crucial question is, are we doing it, is it a part of our everyday lives?

We in New Life teach quite a lot on worship, it is one of what we call our core values, "We are a people of worship". Yet I have to admit for all this emphasis, I'm not sure everyone in our congregation has totally grasped this concept. I usually sit at the front of the church, but if I turn around, I often see people I love and care about, who have problems and difficulties or are needing a breakthrough in some area of their lives, sitting passively during worship. I want to go to them and encourage them, "Don't waste this opportunity, worship, if you want a breakthrough in your life, worship God. Make an effort, a sacrifice Hebrews calls it, (Hebrews 13:15), turn from your problems, shake off lethargy, put your eyes on God and honour Him."

You see, I have found by experience as well as teaching, that worship brings a breakthrough. Worship turns mountains into molehills. I have no need to bind the enemy, if I worship, he is bound, made powerless, (Psalm 149:6-9) I may enter a worship service feeling depressed, fed-up, tired or weary but if I make the effort, my spirit is always lifted. I challenge you to give it a go, try it and experience release in God.

But worship is an awful lot more than what happens in a church service. Worship is also giving, of our time, our gifts, our possessions, our love and also our money. Jarrod teaches us that our tithes and offerings are our ultimate act of worship; many of us need converting in our purses and our wallets. Worship by giving brings release in our finances and our lives. Do you know that even the business world has caught on to this concept and companies are advised to give 10% of their profits to charity if they want to prosper! Where did they get that idea from then?

Worship is also an all day every day happening. It's not just for church, or even during our personal quiet time or when we are playing our music tapes. Of course, all that is good and necessary, but God seeks worshipping hearts, a worship attitude, worship that never ceases. For example, we cannot walk out of a worship service where we have sought to honour and exalt God and begin to talk doubt, fear, complaining and negativity, that would be inconsistent and hypocritical. God asks us to cultivate a heart of gratitude, praise, thankfulness, love and faith. I sincerely believe God responds to our gratitude. When we thank Him for what we have, even though it may be little, He gives us more. It may be old-fashioned, but when we count our blessings, He pours even more into our laps.

I recently heard a lovely story of how God brought release through praise from a young couple who had recently joined our church. Mark and Maria had been married for nine years and were still childless. They had tests and all seemed healthy but still, no baby and they were about to be offered I.V.F. Only Maria was with us at this time and during a service, Isaiah 54:1-3 was read, "Sing O barren woman….burst into song….shout for joy," She had that leap in her spirit, that excitement that says, "This is for you!" and she was determined to take her eyes off her sadness at her childless marriage and consciously and purposely began to praise God every day, to sing and shout His praises. She checked herself constantly at any unbelief or sadness. Mark, the husband, joined us about two weeks after this revelation and to cut a long story short, within weeks, pregnancy was confirmed. Praise God worship has creative, reproducing power!

Psalm 22 tells us that God dwells in our praises.

Psalm 92 says it is a good thing to praise God and it keeps us young and fruitful.

1 Peter 2:9 says it is the reason we are chosen, that we may declare His praises.

John 4:24 says the Father seeks true worshippers.

But far above all, we worship Him because He is worthy.

"Worthy is the Lamb who was slain, to receive power and wealth and wisdom and strength and honour and glory and praise! To Him who sits on the throne and to the Lamb be praise and honour and glory and power forever and ever!"

Revelation 5:12-13

Chapter 27
Calling

One of the things that trouble many people, especially young people, is the calling of God on their lives. Their worries range from "Is this God really calling me?" to "Have I missed the call of God?" and even "Things have not gone well, yet I was sure God called me, did I get it wrong?" Many Christians seem to believe that God places us in a maze and tells us "Right now find my will and woe betides you if you miss it."

But my experience of the calling of God has been rather kinder, clearer and more persistent, especially in the bigger decisions of life, (if not quite so much with those daily little nudges to do something specific there and then, where I believe experience and even trial and error helps.)

I became a Christian at 14 years of age from a non-Christian background. My salvation was very thorough and I was immediately passionate about God and the things of God. One of the values by which I lived my life, even at that age was, "whatever your hand finds to do, do it with all your might". My spiritual upbringing included such wise little nuggets as "saved to serve" and that I had now joined the R.F.A., Ready for Anything, - alright, old-fashioned, but still good! So very early in my Christian life, I knew God had called me to serve Him in some special way.

After marrying David our desire to serve remained and we were involved in almost every area of our church, Sunday school, youth, evangelism, prayer, newsletter and the cleaning teams (excellent training!).

I'm telling you these things to show you that one of the things I have learned is that training and experience begins at home. Even if you are privileged to go to Bible school or need specialist training for your ministry, what you don't or won't do in your home church, you are going to struggle within the place of your calling. I cannot count the number of people who share what they believe is God's word on their lives but who are unwilling to "train" at home, to get their hands dirty in their local church. The best advice to anyone seeking God's will for their lives is, be loyal, committed and reliable in your home church and whatever you are allowed to do (even if it's cleaning the loos) do it excellently. It is God's training ground for you. Understand too, that God is not only training you, He is shaping your character. Gifting without character is a recipe for disaster.

The next lesson I learned through experience is if you genuinely and sincerely want to hear God's will for your life, you cannot miss it. He will not let you. When I am unsure of what God is saying, I ask Him, "Lord you know I am a bit thick at times please don't let me go wrong, confirm your word to me." And I'm not embarrassed especially in life's big decisions, to ask this several times, (remember Gideon and the fleeces) and I prefer to have at least one outside or impartial input. Also in life changing decisions, don't rush, take your time and take counsel from spiritual fathers, preferably with no axe to grind. David and I from our initial calling to Gibraltar, took 5 years to actually go, yes I know that was a bit slow, but what can I say? We were initially reluctant!

And that brings me to my third discovery. If you feel reluctant, inadequate and weak that doesn't mean it isn't God, actually, I would now say to the contrary. I know very few people, if any, in ministry, who don't at times feel totally inadequate and have to rely completely and utterly on God, His calling and anointing to get through. Think of all the people who felt unable and even unwilling in the Bible, Jeremiah, Moses, Esther, and Gideon etc. What excuses they came up with! Very few of us are like Isaiah and say "Here am I, send me," without trembling knees.

Fourthly I would say that being in God's will does not mean that you will have immediate success or that things will be easy. When our family first went to Gibraltar, we had the hardest of times in many areas. But we held on to and remembered God's calling on our lives. We repeated the scriptures He had given us and remembered the way He had led us and the many God-incidences that had brought us to this place. For example, in our first three years there, we had to move house 6 times, through no fault of our own, and at one point were actually homeless with two small children. This was very hard for us because in England, David had had a good job in management with British Steel and we had owned our own house. But as we prayed and sought God, He showed us there was a purpose to all this. Troubling and distressing as times like this are, this is when we grow in God, hear His voice more clearly, pray more fervently, know his supernatural peace and receive Godly provision. The tough times we experienced didn't harm our children either. They grew up knowing even the godly life can be tough but at least it's an adventure and above all, God is faithful.

I have also learned to be in ministry for love of God and for no other reason. Ministry, whether it's teaching Sunday school, leading a cell group, evangelism or leading a church, is very people orientated and I know the Bible puts love for people, especially our brothers, very high. But my experience is that people can be very fickle and I think this was probably the biggest shock and the steepest learning curve when we led our first church. People may love and support you one minute, but are totally capable of abandoning you, accusing you and misunderstanding you the next. David is unfazed by this behaviour, but I, who am much more of a people person, totally struggled and was initially devastated by such behaviour. I regularly wanted to "throw in the towel", until I realised that these people, much as I loved them, had not called me, had not invited me to their country or their city and they owed me nothing. But God had called me, and now I serve because I love Him, He is my focus and He is not fickle, He is faithful. He is my encouragement, support, anointing and success, His love for me never waivers.

And finally, I have learned success comes from God alone. I have often feared failure in ministry and at one particularly difficult time, had spent the morning crying and laying my fears before God. We had been given a certain scripture 3 times in 3 weeks by 3 different people and on this day David returned home not knowing about my current distress, and said," I've been reading that scripture God gave us, in the Good News Bible, listen to what it says," and I leave this precious verse, which has given us so much comfort, with you.

"YOU WILL SUCCEED, not by military might or by your own strength, but by my spirit (says the Lord). Obstacles as great as mountains will disappear before you." Zechariah 4:6-7 (Good News Bible)

Chapter 28
Suffering For Jesus

The church in Great Britain lives in an age of embracing blessing, prosperity and growth. I believe with all my heart that Gods' desire is to bless us, empower us, heal and deliver. God is on our side; we need to grasp this fact. His thoughts are indeed "to give us a hope and a future" (Jeremiah 29:11)

As I was growing up in the church in the late fifties and early sixties, the mentality was rather different and although we knew our God was a good God, we had a "fear not little flock" mentality. The church expected to remain small and suffer; persecution always seemed imminent. At least that is how it seemed to my teenage perspective. And although I rejoice at being free of that mentality, I sometimes wonder, have we thrown the baby out with the bath water. Is there now such an expectation of only blessings, that if we suffer at all, we question, "Where is our God?"

An expectation of only blessing, or should I perhaps say an easy life, is unscriptural and would ultimately lead to a weak immature church.

2 Timothy 3:12 says, "All who desire to live godly in Christ Jesus will suffer".

In Matthew 16:21 Jesus our supreme example revealed that "He must suffer many things". And in 2 Timothy 1:8-9 Paul urged the young Timothy, "Take your share of suffering for the message."

It may be we suffer because we are living and working amongst unbelievers who ridicule, reject and may even persecute us for our faith. It may be, as we seek to live godly, righteous lives before them, we perturb their conscience. This certainly was a real feature of my life as a young Christian, when probably enthusiasm rather than wisdom ruled.

The Bible urges us to bear this undeserved suffering with gladness (Matthew 5:12) (If we suffer because of doing wrong that's another matter and we need to repent and apologise.)

In so many other parts of the world, being a Christian is a dangerous choice. At one time, David and I travelled regularly to North Africa and met parts of the underground church there. We personally knew people beaten, persecuted and restricted because of their faith in Jesus. We can only imagine the true suffering and cost these brothers and sisters pay to believe in Jesus. How light our affliction seems compared to theirs.

But there is another form of suffering that happens to Christians too.

Do you remember when Jesus was in the garden of Gethsemane praying and in agony over his impending torture and death? He said to the Father those historic words, "Everything is possible for you. Take this cup from me. Yet not what I will, but what you will". (Mark 14:36) He chose his Fathers' will before and over his own.

Gethsemane means "oil press". It was the place the olives were crushed and made into olive oil. Now olives are potentially extremely useful, but in their raw state, they have limited use. Never walk into an olive grove, pluck an olive from the tree and eat it, they are inedible. They must first be processed, usually more than once, to draw the bitterness from them. Or they must be pressed to obtain olive oil, which is then so valuable and useful, in the Mediterranean it is thought of as liquid gold.

To reach their potential, olives must be crushed and pressed (persecuted or suffer).

For Jesus to reach his full potential, to redeem mankind, he suffered, was persecuted and hard pressed, his Gethsemane experience was just a part of this process.

For us to reach our potential, to mature in God, to achieve full usefulness, it is necessary that we are pressed, crushed, persecuted and suffer. That we reach a place in our lives where we cry, "Abba, Father, I am in a place of great pain, if possible I ask you to remove this from my life, but not my will but yours be done".

Going to Gibraltar 40 years ago was very much this sort of experience for us. It was not our choice, it caused heartache, pain and tears, but we ultimately knew it was God's will and that peace, fulfilment and reaching our potential, lay in obedience.

In our early years of ministry there, through no fault of our own, we became homeless. It was a very difficult time and obviously, we talked it over with God. We believed we were in His will and purpose and so what had gone wrong? God revealed that we were being beaten for the light. (Exodus 27:20, Leviticus 24:20) Olive oil for lamps must be particularly pure, any impurity will cause the lamp to smoke and flicker or even extinguish. This brought peace of mind, we were being hard pressed to reach our full, long-term potential in God.

I have heard recently of people who have chosen the will of God over careers and promotion and have chosen at a crucial time in their lives to go to Bible School. Their testimony is that long-term careers did not suffer as they put God's will before their own. Others have relinquished love, relationship and marriage because the one they loved was unsaved, didn't share their calling or simply because they knew it wasn't God's will, painful - even agonising choices.

Choosing the will of God above our own is not easy and such choices can cause much pain and suffering but, as the apostle Paul declares, are ultimately worth it.

"I consider that our present sufferings are not worth comparing with the glory that will be revealed in us." Romans 8:18

Chapter 29
Prayer Principles

Prayer is so often fraught with mixed emotions. We want to pray and understand that "prayer precedes power" and that "prayer changes things." We want this power and authority, this intimate relationship with God and yet there is the fleshly side of our lives that we struggle to discipline. But there are some nitty-gritty down to earth principles that make prayer easy and accessible but above all effective.

The first principle is that if we want to see answers, we need to pray with fervour. James 4:2 says, "You do not have because you do not ask." The word "ask" here is not a half-hearted request but literally means, to be zealous for, to pursue ardently, to desire eagerly and intensely. This is the type of prayer that has power.

My second principle is to persevere. When Paul asked God only three times to remove his thorn in the flesh, it was not a pattern but an exception. By and large, the Bible encourages us to persevere, amusingly even "to pester" in prayer, until we receive our petition. (Luke 18:2-7)

The third principle is we need to be convinced in our hearts that we have a good God who wants to bless us. Romans 8.32 reassures us "He who did not spare his own son, but gave him up for us all- how will he not also along with him graciously (freely) give us all things." And "all things" means God is willing to bless the most trivial and intimate things in our lives. David and I pray for parking places, shopping bargains and thank Him for every small blessing He pours into our lives. I know it sounds naïve but God will meet you exactly where you expect.

The fourth principle is to fulfil the "ifs". We in New Life Church are in the middle of five weeks prayer and fasting. We are seeking to fulfil the "if" in 2 Chronicles 7:14, "If my people who are called by my name will humble themselves and pray and seek my face and turn from their wicked ways, then will I hear from heaven and will forgive their sins and heal their land." When we are seeking God in prayer it is important to check our lives with the word of God, to make sure we are walking in obedience, not to earn Gods favour but to remove anything that might block it. For example, 1 Peter 3:7, advises husbands to love and respect their wives so their prayers are not hindered!

Fifthly and crucially, for prayer to be powerfully effective, and to be life, church and city changing, we need to hear from God. We can use His general word (logos) and pray according to scripture but even more powerful is when we receive, as we seek Him, a specific (or rhema) word. Two years ago, after 7 months of chronic back pain following a fall and after a difficult and frightening consultation with my GP, God gave me the word, "You have turned the corner". Within a few days I had stopped all pills and was totally out of pain.

At the end of last year, I spoke at a women's conference in Scotland. As I arrived a young woman told me she had heard me speak almost 2 years ago. At this time, in response to the teaching, God had challenged her she was not fighting sufficiently for her backslidden teenage daughter. When she went home, her husband met her at the door, with that same conviction. Together they began to fervently hold on to God and within two weeks their daughter was back walking with the Lord!

On another occasion, a woman in our fellowship shared with me that her daughter in America was pregnant with seriously conjoined twin girls. During the prayer meeting, God prompted me to pray, along with the grandmother, that unless a miracle was to happen, would God take these babies to Himself. Two weeks later, I asked how things were and was told her daughter had indeed miscarried the babies. But sad as this was, she then told me a beautiful story. During the miscarriage, her daughter had a near-death experience, during which, strangely, she saw two beautiful healthy little boys running towards her, arms outstretched, calling "Mummy, Mummy". When she revived, the hospital staff informed her that her babies had not been little girls after all but had been little boys! What an extraordinary good God we have who not only prompts us how to pray to spare unnecessary pain, but miraculously comforts a young mother in her grief that her babies are safe with Him

And my final effective prayer principle, be grateful. Psalm 100, "give thanks to Him and praise His name for the Lord is good and His love endures forever."

SECTION 5

The Mature Years

Chapter 30
How Old Is Old?

I had a terrible shock some years ago. We had decided in our church to do a series on lifestyle. Jarrod, my younger son, who was our associate minister at the time, was handing out subjects for us all to speak on. In the past when we have done this type of subject, I have always done such things as Marriage or Parenting or even Honouring Parents. But this time as the subjects came up, Jarrod said to me "Mum, I would like you to do 'Maturing'"! Although I accepted the subject calmly, I wanted to say, "What do I know about Maturing!"

You see here is my problem; I was at that time 59 years old. In my heart I feel 25, I feel fit and well, and a lot of the time I don't think I even look my age. Of course, that could have something to do with the fact that I refuse to wear my specs except for reading and driving! If you are getting on a bit you should try this, it's like airbrushing a photo, - excellent! But on other days, I look in the mirror and there is my precious mother staring back at me! Being given this subject forced me to consider my age and "where I was at" in my life.

There are pluses to being older. I feel I know myself better and am more confident. I am less upset by the opinion of others, having learned I can never please everyone. I have proved God over and over again in my life. I know that current problems will pass. But where have all the years gone! It seems such a short while ago, I was a young married woman with babies and soon I will be a pensioner! Even the very fact that I talk in this way proves my age; the young don't talk like this!

In many ways, I am very blessed, in that I have so few regrets, and those I have are very minor. I came to God aged 14 years from a non-Christian background and I have walked with Him ever since. I have had a good, strong and happy marriage. Together we have reared two wonderful sons, Jason and Jarrod, and God and His service has been the centre of our family, giving us great adventures together. I realise how blessed I am, because this can so often be the time for regrets, what we didn't do, what we didn't achieve, the opportunities that never seemed to occur.

A further cause of pain at this age is to see beloved parents struggling with old age and senility, sharing their pain but also feeling that you are potentially looking at your own future in twenty or so year's time, which no longer feels that far away.

Many friends of a similar age also have the pain of grown-up children who have turned away from God, bringing its own fears and the worry of "Could we have done things differently?"

At this time of life, we should all be feeling more financially secure but sadly in this day of failing pensions, many of us don't even have that comfort.

Even the Bible can be depressing about old age! Read Ecclesiastes 12 preferably in the Living Waters translation, probably written by Solomon in his old age, showing the futility of life without God. Even he, with all his wives and concubines says "Desire fails"! What heartache, having waning sexual desire to add to the list! (Don't make me laugh; my bladder muscles aren't so reliable recently!)

But I have decided to refuse old age, its frailties and weaknesses. Instead I take as my examples and role models, people who are keen-minded, humorous and relevant to the end, such people as John Mills, the Queen Mum and an old brother in our church called Syd who rode his bike to church until 3 months before his death, aged 96, deaf as a post but with a teenage spirit. We still miss his laugh.

Deuteronomy 33:25 "As are your days, so shall your strength be."

Isaiah 40:31 "They that wait on the Lord shall renew their strength."

Deuteronomy 34:7 of Moses aged 120 years, "His eyes were not weak nor his strength gone."

Psalm 92:14 " They will still bear fruit in old age, they will stay fresh and green."

Psalm 103:5 "So that your youth is renewed like the eagles."

These are the words I choose to believe, these are the words I speak over my life when tempted to fear old age. I remind myself of the many men and women in the Bible who were all fruitful and influential in old age, who affected the next generation positively, encouraging them to stand on their shoulders spiritually and to reach higher. I think of Moses, who led a nation, Noah who saved his family, what would Elisha be without Elijah, Ruth without Naomi, even Eli helped Samuel recognise the voice of God, Mordecai advised Esther, David collected the material for the temple which his son then built, and Paul nurtured Timothy.

Yes, I am far from finished, I am not old, I am mature and we are all told to strive for maturity, or another word, perfection. (Hebrews 6:1) I remind myself of words spoken over my life not yet fully fulfilled. I believe the next phase will be more fruitful than the former.

I plan to be like Caleb, strong and vigorous and with the Lord's help, ready for battle, to take a new, long promised land. (Joshua 14:10-15)

So you ask me, how old is old? I know 30-year-olds who are old and 90-year-olds who are young, so I don't know. All I know is, I'm not old, are you?

Chapter 31
"I know That My Redeemer Lives"

David and I regularly have to make long, rather boring motorway journeys. Because we are busy people, we try to utilise this time as much as we can. We listen to teaching tapes or worship tapes, we take the time to pray together (eyes open of course!), the one who isn't driving may use it to study or go through teaching notes. But a few months ago, on one such journey, I made a startling discovery.

I was concerned about one of my relatives, who we will call James. He doesn't know God and has had a difficult and often sad life. I have spoken to him of God many times over the years and I know that my life has at times challenged him, but his response has always been negative, at times vehemently so. James had just been passing through yet another difficult time and in my head on this particular journey, I was rehearsing what I would love to say to him and what I would wish his response to be. I'm sure many of us do this when people we love and care for seem unable to see the wonder and joy of the Gospel.

I wanted to say to him, "Just suppose, just suppose for a while, that I am right. That there is a God, a God who cares about us, a God who cares so much He actually wants a relationship with us. To make this possible, He sends His only Son Jesus to die in our place, to take the punishment for our sins and to make us one with Him again. A God who helps, supports and encourages in this life but who also gives us eternal life with Him, a God who has defeated death for us. If I am right dear James, I have won and you have lost. I have won because God has so blessed me in this life, He has been with me in the dark places, He has filled my life with His love, joy and peace. While you have struggled with hurt, sadness and rejection alone. If I am right, when I die I will know eternal life with Jesus in heaven, and you my dear James, what will your eternity hold?"

Having been through this scenario in my head, I began to think the unthinkable and all it took was a matter of seconds. What if he was right and I was wrong? Supposing there is no God, no God who loves and cares and helps, no God to deal with death, no hope, and no future. Had I thrown my whole life away on a God who doesn't exist? This God, who supposedly isn't there but has blessed my life so much, has healed me, answered my prayers, spoken to me over and over again, given me wisdom for life, guided and directed my ways, given me abundant, joyful life, filled me with His Holy Spirit, who makes my heart dance, who excites me, who has given me laughter lines! If you, dear relative, are right and I am wrong, what of eternity; nothingness for both of us? And this is when I made this most startling discovery, that even if James is right, just supposing there is no God, I still had not lost, I was still the winner. Why? Because in this life I have known such joy in Jesus, such companionship with Him, I have known acceptance, freedom from guilt and fear, He has given me such adventures, I have no regrets, I have not lost, I am still a winner right or wrong! My trust in Jesus has made me twice a winner and your unbelief; James has made you twice a loser.

As I briefly contemplated this most awful thought, no God, no heaven, no eternity, I sensed something happening deep within me. A bubble of pure joy, assurance and laughter rose through my ribcage into my throat, a smile spread across my face and into my mouth came those wondrous words, "I KNOW that my Redeemer lives and He shall stand at last on the earth, And after my skin is destroyed this I KNOW, That in my flesh I shall see God, Whom I shall see for myself and my eyes shall behold and not another, How my hearts yearns within me!" Job 19:25

How privileged we are to have that deep assurance in our spirits, even in the face of opposition and negativity, to know like Job, at times of great pressure in our lives, when no one can tell us why this is happening, that God is there. He is on our side, He will not fail us. We may lose the odd battle, but because of Jesus we have already won the war, no matter what happens, we are on the winning side.

As we seek in our lives to give an account of what we believe, to live our every day ordinary life as a testimony to the living God before friends, relatives and work colleagues, may everything that we say, do and are declare with assurance;

"I KNOW THAT MY REDEEMER LIVES"

Chapter 32
Journey's End

"O death where is your sting, O grave, where is your victory"

So says I Corinthians 15:55 (NKJ), yet I have in the past, struggled with a fear of the grave. The fear first began some twenty odd years ago, when each year for 3 years a close member of my family died. It was also the first time I had experienced bereavement so intimately. Having returned from the third funeral, I began to wake in the night with terrible nightmares of being buried alive. The fear was exacerbated by living in Gibraltar, where the dead are buried within 24 hours. A friend's father went to work in the morning, died and by teatime was in the grave! I am embarrassed by this fear because I'm a Christian and understand, and believe, Jesus died to defeat death on our behalf. With a deep conviction, I know I should not fear. But the enemy knows exactly our weakest areas and times to do battle, doesn't he, and it was during the night, when often spiritually vulnerable, that the attacks would come and I would wake sweating and trembling.

I dealt with this awful fear by reading God's word, particularly Psalms, through prayer and praise and, like King David in Psalm 42:5, by giving myself a good talking to. I reminded myself that God, who had never failed me in life, certainly would not fail me in death. Although it took several weeks, the strength of the fear was broken.

But then, just a few years ago, the death of a dear friend

tremendously excited me.

Lucy was a beautiful Christian lady, in every sense of that word. She loved her husband and her children deeply; they, and Jesus were the centre of her world. Each week we prayed together and became quite close. Her spiritual enthusiasm was inspiring. She had known some health problems, but was still quite active and only in her early 70's.

Only in hindsight did we truly realise what had happened. Over the period of a few weeks, this gentle, unassuming woman became more and more excited about the things of God and particularly at the prospect of heaven. David had been doing a series on heaven and during this time, Lucy's "Amens" and "Praise God" became more and more voluble as she raised her hands and punched the air in enthusiasm.

Also, Jarrod had returned to Hull and was working with us. He often talked about his vision and heart for revival in our nation. Lucy became a great encouragement to him. "I am so excited at the things God is doing in you. I believe you have a great future in Jesus and will see great things. I am with you and praying for you, go for it!" she would tell him.

Then one week, we had a guest speaker who said "finally" several times before he finished. Lucy had stood up at the first "finally" and stood beside him, explaining God had told her to dance around the church. She had to stand there several minutes before he "finally" finished. Under normal circumstances, I might have suggested she sit with me on the front row while he ended, but this was so unlike Lucy, I knew this was a "God moment".

As the speaker ended, she began to dance around the church. Several of the women, unwilling for her to dance alone, joined her. Her joy and excitement in God was obvious and infectious.

Just two days later on Tuesday morning, she went into her kitchen to make a cup of tea, had a massive heart attack and died.

It was then it became clear to us all, that her mounting excitement was God preparing her for "home". I love travelling and I can only compare it to when I have booked a holiday abroad and am so excited about the impending journey and destination. Had God been showing her His travel brochure, could she see heaven and the mansion prepared for her? Was she anticipating those streets of gold?

That old hymn leapt into my mind.

"O Beulah land, sweet Beulah land, as on the highest mount I stand,

I look away across the sea, where mansions are prepared for me,

And view the shining glory shore, my heaven my home for evermore."

I understand there is still pain in death, particularly the awful pain of separation. It is still the ultimate journey, the great unknown, the great faith adventure. But I aspire to this death, where I glimpse more clearly my God and Saviour. Where I see heaven, my eternal home, where I move from this world to the next, not with fear, trepidation, anxiety or even resignation but with joy, enthusiasm and excitement.

The year that Lucy died, we as a church family lost three of our patriarchs and Jarrod wrote a song in their memory, called "Journey's End". Here is what he said, on the album, in dedicating this song to them.

"Several dear friends and church members found their journey's end in Jesus over the last few years. I'm not sure if they can hear this song- but I hope it reminds those left behind, that we go to a far, far better place, where pain and tears, sickness and fear is wiped away."

"Tenderly your love has brought me, to the gates of heaven.

You have been my way, my journey, and now

Jesus, you're my journey's end." (Jarrod Cooper)

SECTION 6

When Storms Rage

Chapter 33
It Is Alright Part 1

At the beginning of 2005, God dropped a word into my heart that has been a lifeline throughout the year. When I first heard it, I had no idea how precious and important it would become over the months that followed.

That word is found in 2 Kings 4:23, and then again in verse 26. "It is alright" or in other translations, "All is well". It was spoken by the Shunammite woman, whose much loved and wanted little son had died after a brief illness. Initially, she said it to her husband and then to the prophet Elisha when she sought his help. Words of optimism, trust, hope and faith in her God and His prophet, because patently at that point, humanly speaking, all was not well.

In January, when God first spoke these words to my heart, the world was reeling from the effect of that awful tsunami and the tens of thousands of deaths it caused. On a church and personal level, there were problems and serious illnesses, so these words were immediately precious, comforting and hope renewing, to have God remind us, that in the midst of life's worst storms, was the great I AM and by faith, we could declare, "It is alright".

But as 2005 unfolded, it became obvious even on a world level, that this was one exceptionally troubled year. The earth itself moaned, groaned and was deeply troubled. Floods, fires, storms, tornadoes, hurricanes and earthquakes shook our world.

Terrorism again raised its dreadful head even in our little nation, close to home, in safe secure England, bringing with it fear, suspicion, blame and prejudice.

On a family level, the storms have sought to shake our hearts. My lovely, funny, courageous sister-in-law, fighting ovarian cancer for the last two years, has now been diagnosed terminally ill. My younger brother suffered through an acrimonious divorce and struggled enormously to rebuild his life.

A 29-year-old young woman from a family we had pastored in Gibraltar was involved in a serious car accident here in Britain. We sat by her bed, with her warm, loving and dignified family as the doctor declared her dead. What can you say, what can you do but cry with them and in your heart declare, "It is alright", He is still in control, all is not lost, we have a hope.

Just a few weeks later, I sat by the bed of another dying woman, this time at a good age and after a long and full life. But the pain was just as intense because this woman was my own mother. I found it hard to immediately mourn for her because her mind and her body had for some time failed her. I couldn't wish her back like that, but over the following weeks, oh how I miss the woman she was, our days out together in Nottingham, our shopping trips and coffee mornings, her inner strength, humour and determination.

And so this troubled year rolled on with wars, famines and more earthquakes. Hurricanes turned parts of America into a third world country, bird flu threatened a pandemic. It would be so easy to have "our hearts fail us through fear".

I am guilty of wanting a peaceful life of ease, of wanting to "lie down in green pastures" and "be led by still waters", but in that very same Psalm 23, David reminds us "Yea tho' I walk through the valley of the shadow of death, you are with me".

Another of my favourites, Psalm 91, talks of God's special love, protection and keeping over those who trust in Him. I quote it to myself often, but right there in verse 15 it says, "I will be with him in trouble." Therefore we will have troubles! Storms will disrupt our lives. We will walk through the valley of the shadow of death. But through it all, the one constant, the unchanging and unmoveable, the One from whom we can never be separated, our eternal hope, our rock and harbour, is God.

I end with the words of this song by my son Jarrod, based on Psalm 91. As I listened to this song in January 2005, I wept for the thousands killed by the tsunami, not realising how many more tears would be shed that year.

"You, tho' the mountains quake, And fall into the sea,
Still your love stands firm
And you, tho' the earth give way
You're an ever-present help
And your words endure throughout the generations
You are my hiding place, The lifter of my head
You have heard my cry, And you, tho' a thousand fall
Your hand remains on me
And your faithfulness will be my shield and fortress
I give you praise, Ancient of Days, I give you glory,
I honour you, faithful and true, Lord Almighty."
(Jarrod Cooper)

Whatever this year may bring, whether the sun shines out of a cloudless sky, or whether storms disrupt our lives, let us say by faith in our God, with the Shunammite woman, "IT IS ALRIGHT"

Chapter 34
It Is Alright Part 2

In the last chapter I wrote about the storms that so often rock our lives, be they world issues or much closer to home. And how faith inspiring it is to be able to declare, like the Shunammite woman after the death of her little boy, "It is alright", God is still in control. (2 Kings 4)

It is human nature when we are going through tough times, especially when it is a prolonged storm, or one storm after another, to ask the question, why? "Lord, why am I suffering in this way?" "Why can't I come through this situation quickly?" "Is there a reason?" "What have I done or not done?" Sometimes we even ask this question when we see a brother or sister tossed by storms and here, I suggest, is where it can get a bit dangerous. Because sometimes "I don't know" is the godly and spiritually mature answer, but we are often unhappy with this and want to speak into a situation, bring understanding and discernment.

In John 9:2 in the story of the man who was blind from birth, the disciples wanted a reason for his condition, someone to blame. Jesus told them, no one has sinned, this is so God's glory may be revealed.

Again in the story of Job and all the distress, pain and suffering he endured, his friends asked, "What have you done?" They reasoned, no one would suffer like this unless they had committed huge sins. The real truth was that God was so proud of Job and boasted to Satan about Job's love, dedication, faithfulness and righteousness, so

Satan asked permission to test these virtues with trials.

If we always try to bring reasons for storms, especially when speaking into the lives of others, we can cause so much pain, guilt and rejection. As I have talked with people with prolonged difficulties, the pain they feel at being accused of sin, unforgiveness, or lack of faith, only adds to their suffering, and I would suggest is best dealt with alongside church leadership, someone in authority and spiritually mature, who by investing into their lives has earned the right to sensitively, and lovingly bring these insights.

I believe our response to a problem is more important than asking the reason. Some people turn away from God in difficult times as they did in John 6:66 when they found the words of Jesus too hard to accept. The disciples found His words difficult to handle too, but their answer to His, "Will you leave me too?" was a good example to us in hard times or when we don't understand. They said, "Where shall we go, you have the words of eternal life", rather than become angry, bitter or self-pitying, all of which can exacerbate the problem and certainly doesn't solve it.

Romans 5:3 challenges us to "Rejoice in suffering", how tough is that?

James 1.3 tells us to consider trials pure joy because they build maturity in us. None of us want to remain Christian infants and unfortunately ease does not cause us to grow, trials and storms of all sorts do!

Do good godly people suffer then? Yes of course. Probably the best example I can give is in 2 Corinthians 11:23-29, where we find a list of the apostle Paul's sufferings. (Would you get into a boat with Paul? Three times shipwrecked!) We also know that Paul had some long-standing weakness that, in spite of asking several times, God refused to take away, but rather strengthened Paul through it (2 Corinthians 12:7). Paul's response to the storms in his life are also a big example to us, "We are hard pressed on every side but not crushed, perplexed but not in despair; persecuted but not abandoned; struck down but not destroyed."(2 Corinthians 4:8-9) In a nutshell he was saying, this is tough but we will not give up, still we will trust in God.

It is in hard times, too, that we prove our faithfulness. Anyone can walk well when the sun is shining, but when storm clouds cross our skies, we live the godly life simply because it is the right thing to do. We continue to read God's word, even if it is only crying over Psalms. We continue to pray, even if we are reduced to spreading out our problems before God and saying, "Please help," as Hezekiah did (2 Kings 19:14-19). We continue to worship, even if it is the biggest sacrifice we have ever made (Hebrews 13.15). We continue to fellowship, because we need, even more at this point in our lives, the love and motivation of being in God's house, with God's people, sitting under His word. We continue to live the godly life, yes for our own sake, but also for the sake of our testimony, because it is at this time more than any other, that the world watches our response.

Certainly, it is a good thing to ask the Holy Spirit to show us if we have in any way caused the problem. To close every loophole we may have given the enemy in our lives, to confess and repent of any sin, unforgiveness, disobedience or foolishness, to align our lives with the word of God, to check our attitudes, to ask for God's wisdom in our everyday ordinary lives.

There is a point also if we genuinely feel this is the enemy and that we have dealt with all we can, that we like Shammah, stand "in our field of lentils" and say to the enemy "so far but no further". This is God's ground. 2 Samuel 23:12

Declaring the word of God over our lives also has great power to sustain us, encourage faith and raise our eyes to Him.

"We know that in all things God works for the good of those who love Him…What then shall we say in response to this? If God is for us, who can be against us?…Who shall separate us from the love of Christ? Shall trouble or hardship or persecution or famine or nakedness or danger or sword?….No in all these things we are more than conquerors through Him who loved us. For I am convinced that …nothing…will be able to separate us from the love of God." (Romans 8:28)

Chapter 35
It Is Alright Part 3

When we have difficult times in our lives, no one will pretend it is easy. It is indeed difficult to "rejoice in suffering" and "to be joyful in tribulations", but there is no doubt in my mind at all, that times of storms can be the most precious and fruitful of our lives.

My testimony is that during the darkest times of my life, I have heard God the clearest. And the words He has spoken into my life at these times have remained indelibly printed on my heart and at later trials; I have pulled them up from my spirit and encouraged myself with them.

Many years ago, during a period of about a year, the church David and I belonged to went through very hard times. People were dying every few weeks. Sometimes older people died but also two teenagers and a young woman in her early twenties. It didn't seem to make any difference if we fasted and prayed, still, they died. Others died very suddenly, giving us no time to seek God's face. The young woman in her early twenties came home from work, told her mother she felt unwell, lay on the settee, and died. It was a deeply troubling time and we all began to ask, "Who is next?" We were fearful for our children. It came to a head on Good Friday, David had been to the service and came home and said that the wife of one of the elders had died. She had been ill for just two weeks with leukaemia.

I began to cry and ask, "What have we done, why has God removed His hand from us, have we as a church sinned, has God left us?" No sooner were the words out of my mouth, when David, who was by now in bed and reading the Bible, said: "Listen to this". At that exact moment, he had reached Hebrews 13:5 in the Amplified Bible.

"I will not in any way fail you, nor give you up, nor leave you without support. I will not, I will not, I will not in any degree leave you helpless, nor forsake nor let you down, nor relax my hold on you, "ASSUREDLY NOT!"

On the next Sunday morning, Easter Day, one of the elders prophesied and there in the middle were those same words, " I will never leave you or forsake you."

I began to cry yet again! But this time with joy and relief, we knew with a deep unshakeable certainty that God had spoken, He had not left us and He never would. What caused all the deaths? Only God knows and of course it doesn't lessen the tragedy for those families immediately involved, but His comfort, reassurance and hope filled our hearts. I have never forgotten that promise, that deep assurance, our God does not abandon us.

During our early years in Hull, after a brief honeymoon period, we hit difficult times. It was an extremely painful period in our lives. But God had called us to this City and we were determined to obey God's calling on our lives. As we walked through this time of great hurt and rejection, God spoke into our lives over and over again. Almost on a daily basis, God reassured us of His protection and calling. Isaiah 41:8-20 became especially precious. He spoke to us of His future plans for our lives and ministry and reassured us we would not fail. Zechariah 4:6, in the Good News Bible reads, "You will succeed…by my Spirit."

It is at times like this, isn't it, that our quiet times with God, prayer and reading the word, are by no means a chore, or duty, or something to be fitted into our daily routine. Intimate times with our heavenly Father become a joy, a necessity, we cannot get into His presence quick enough, to pour our hearts out to Him and receive His reassurance. Eighteen years later, we are still in Hull! (We continue to live near the city of Hull, although now retired from full-time ministry. But we served the church there for 26 years until our late retirement in 2013.)

Another quite different example happened when we were on holiday in Turkey. We had taken a sea trip and the return journey proved to be an absolute nightmare! As soon as we left the harbour, our little boat hit huge seas. Many of us were very distressed, fearful, sick, drenched to the skin and desperate for dry land. Naturally, we began to ask God to calm the seas and to get us home safely. All I can tell you is, the sea did not become calm and we endured two hours of great discomfort, but what God did do was calm my heart to the extent that David and I were able to comfort and reassure other people. So much so that the next day talking to other passengers about our horrendous trip and mentioning that we had prayed, they said they had actually noticed how calm and at peace I had become. God did not calm the storm in the sea, but He did indeed calm the storm in my heart so that even others noticed.

So many other stories I could tell you of how God has brought us through life's storms. My son Jason worked for a year in Afghanistan as an aid worker at the climax of their problems. Then he did another year in the Kosovo area during their difficulties. He really should write a book on how God protected, shielded, undertook, guided and provided.

No, I cannot bring myself to pray for trials, but when they come, they can indeed be blessed times. In my life, I want stories and testimonies, not only of how God touched the lives of others, but how He is my deliverer, my rock, my harbour. But if we never know need, how can we know His provision? If we are never sick, how can we experience His healing? If we never mourn, how can we know His comfort? If we are never in danger, how can we experience His protection?

Let us remember, in our storms, trials, valleys and difficulties, with God on our side, "It is indeed alright!"

Chapter 36
Hope Does Not Disappoint

In March 2005, David and I handed over the senior leadership of the church we had been serving for 17 years to our younger son, Jarrod and his wife, Vicky. It wasn't that we felt we had no more to give, on the contrary, a prophecy spoken over us several years before, said God is not into retirement but refirement and we looked forward with eager anticipation to the opportunities that God would open up. (We still work full time in New Life, but as associates, and are as busy as ever, if not more!)

Around this time, a minister's wife gave me a prophecy. She had a picture of me in slippers and God told her to say, "She needs to take those slippers off and put her shoes on because she's going places." I embraced this, already sensing God had more for David and I to accomplish.

But isn't it strange, how often things don't go to plan or turn out how we expect, how often we have to fight to receive the fulfilment of God's word spoken over us?

In July 2006, I had a fall which caused a back injury. A long trip to Colombia, 28 hours door to door each way, exacerbated the problem and several months of extreme pain ensued. An initial wrong diagnosis didn't help either. The exercises I was enthusiastically doing, instead of helping the pain, compounded the problem. Of course, I went forward for prayer and we prayed, in fact, we blessed it, cursed it, bound it, released it and anointed it. I confessed sins I'm not even sure I had committed, anything to break the power of this debilitating pain.

Jarrod came to the house to pray for me one day and advised me to treat this pain as a spiritual attack because the illness had gripped me just as God was opening fresh doors of ministry. (In spite of the pain, I have been able to fulfil every appointment, praise God.) Nevertheless, this was still a very difficult time. On one level, it was embarrassing. I am a leader and a leaders wife, where was my faith? Secondly, because the pain fluctuated, as I improved and people asked how I was, I declared, "Bless God, I'm coming through it," only to re-enter another period of pain. Thirdly, I genuinely believe God is still in the business of healing and I was seriously frustrated. It was also a difficult time because I have always declared, "I don't do sick".

But as always, God used this period to deal with issues in my life and to grow me. Unfortunately, it's in the tough times we mature the most. He taught me humility, patience and endurance, not to give up in prayer but to be persistent. He taught me empathy for those who are sick and in pain, and also that God truly is our strength and help. I missed only one meeting in 7 months of pain, and as, drugged to the eyeballs, I went to celebrate with others His goodness, God never failed to bless, encourage and reassure me, "Do not fear, I am still in control."

Fear had formed an important part of the illness and several times I had to rebuke the emotion that rose up and gripped me, as the enemy tried to tell me, this was it, this was now my life.

One week in my U.C.B. reading, God gave me Jeremiah 29:11 and the commentary said, "Do you feel trapped in an impossible situation you cannot seem to change or escape?" And that was exactly how I felt. With tears, I admitted to God my wavering faith, but that I knew he was my hope and my future.

To confirm this renewed hope, on the next Sunday Jarrod spoke from Hebrews 6:12-15, about how we often need patience to receive and to inherit the promises, just as Abraham did.

Then he moved to verse 19, "We have this hope as an anchor for the soul, firm and secure. It enters the inner sanctuary behind the curtain, where Jesus, who went before us, has entered on our behalf."

I saw my hope, my frail, tiny bit of hope, crawl through that curtain into the inner sanctuary and say to Jesus, "Please remember me, I'm still in pain." And when we are too low, too in pain to pray for ourselves, when we are rock bottom, when all we have is hope, Jesus intercedes on our behalf.

Just a few weeks later, after quite a negative talk to my doctor about chronic, incurable back conditions and yet again having to rebuke the fear this caused in my heart, the very next day, although still in pain, I began to experience waves of peace and a deep sense that God was saying, "You have turned the corner." I stopped taking all medication and by the end of the week, was greatly improved. 3 months later, I have nothing more than a slight weakness that reminds me, don't abuse your back.

At times in those 7 months, I reminded God of that prophecy, "she needs to put her shoes on, she's going places." I have never worn slippers so much in my life as during that time!

Jeremiah 29:11 "I know the plans I have for you, plans to prosper you and not to harm you, plans to give you a hope and a future."

Also translates, "Will restore your fortunes" or "a future of success, NOT of suffering".

Whatever your pain today, let hope, no matter how frail, crawl through that curtain where Jesus entered and intercedes on our behalf.

Romans 5:5 "Suffering produces perseverance, perseverance, character and character hope and hope does not disappoint us."

SECTION 7

Submission

Chapter 37
Submission

To submit is probably one of the hardest instructions within scripture because it means denying my own will and desires and obeying or submitting to the will of others. To submit takes courage and a deeply spiritual heart that understands that God is in charge, even when we are submitting to other humans, and that in submission is power.

But do I believe in submission even when asked to do something that could endanger or damage? – Well, I suppose the simple answer is – "No, I don't", but having said that, Sarah submitted to Abraham when he was being less than a man of God, and asked her to hide the fact that they were married to protect himself.

Genesis 12:11 – "When he was about to cross the border into Egypt, he said to his wife Sarai, "You are a beautiful woman."

Genesis 12:12 – "When the Egyptians see you, they will assume that you are my wife, and so they will kill me and let you live."

Genesis 12:13 – "Tell them that you are my sister; then because of you, they will let me live and treat me well." [Good News Bible]

She obeyed and God protected her, so perhaps in such circumstances submission would follow seeking God's guidance.

I also believe there are times when we must disregard the law. Let me explain. Some months ago, I read that it may become illegal for a minister of religion to refuse to bless the union of homosexuals. David declared, and I totally back him, "I will go to prison before I ever do that." I don't believe it's law yet and I don't envisage it happening simply because other faiths, that the government is afraid of, would also refuse to submit.

I remember as a newly saved teenager, going home from a meeting with red eyes. My parents were already concerned with what they saw as my religious fanaticism. As a parent, I later understood their concerns. Anyway, red eyes were the final straw for my father and he forbade me from going to church again. (Who or what was making his daughter cry?)

All that next day my young heart planned rebellion, justifying that this was my spiritual life in danger. That evening was the Youth Meeting and strangely but wisely, I sat reading when my father came home from work, instead of rushing around to get ready for Youth.

My father asked why I wasn't going out. I reminded him that he had forbidden me. – "It's alright, - you can go," he replied. I can only believe that God had tussled with his heart that day. But at least I had been spared argument and rebellion, and I did learn a strong lesson that I have never forgotten.

When we quietly submit, God works, protects, and persuades on our behalf.

I also recall not submitting to my husband, which I later regretted.

David is a very easy-going man, there is very little he tells me to do or not do. But in our early marriage "selling parties" in the home were popular and I wanted to host one. David said he didn't mind how many girlfriends I had around, but don't invite them to sell to them, - just invite them for fun. I disobeyed this and went ahead with my party, which went fine. But afterwards the trouble I had collecting the money and with faulty goods was a nightmare, and again I learned a lesson I have never forgotten.

Refusing to submit brings consequences and regrets!

I have learned, especially in times of big decisions, or sometimes problems, to hide in my husband's authority and find peace in my heart. But when I told my husband what I wanted to write about this month, he chuckled! I guess he thought with my knowledge and understanding of the subject; it was going to be a short article!

I want to speak about the "S" word, that word that can intimidate the serious Christian, especially women, in our western society. I want us to think about "Submission".

An airline executive said, "All we have to offer is service, and that is very hard to teach because no one wants to be thought of as a servant."

We live in a world that tells us, no - shouts at us, that we are all equal, submit to no one, rebel, speak out, have your say, do it your way. As women we receive the same education as men, may enter any profession and are deemed by many to be the more intelligent gender. Submission does not always come naturally!

Yet lack of submission, respect and honour is at the root of so many of our world's problems.

Children do not want to submit to parents. Employees do not want to submit to employers. Criminals do not want to submit to the law. Wives do not want to submit to their husbands. The congregation does not want to submit to church leaders and nation will not submit to nation. Yet the book by which we live our Christian lives tells us over and over again "Submit".

Jesus, our supreme example, submitted his will to the Fathers. In the Garden of Gethsemane, in torment over his immediate future and sweating great drops of blood, he made a decision and declared, "Father, not my will but yours." His submission saved us; he chose not to do it his way, but the Fathers way and saved the world.

1Peter 3:5-6 tells us "Submit …. and do not fear". What do we fear in submission? Being walked over, taken advantage of, being thought inferior, losing control. Yet the Bible teaches us that in the issues of the Kingdom, the reverse is true. There is blessing, strength, release and authority in submission.

Do you remember the centurion, "I am a man under authority"(in submission)? But because he was under authority, it gave him the power to say to his soldiers "go" or "come" and he would be obeyed. He recognised the same submission and authority in Jesus and his servant was healed. (Luke 7:1-10)

Esther's submission to Mordecai, her Uncle, saved the Jewish nation and empowered her as a woman. So many times in the Bible, we see people submit and become "someone", often greater than the one to whom they submitted. Elisha submitted to Elijah, Samuel submitted to Eli and Timothy submitted to Paul and they were released and became stronger because of it.

Yet I don't believe the Bible teaches us to always blindly and silently submit. Esther discussed the issue with her uncle, even Jesus revealed his heart and his fears to the Father, yet their attitude remained submissive.

Do you really want submissive children? Give them a voice, especially as they get older. Listen to what they are saying and don't be too embarrassed or rigid to readjust your opinion. Children often speak a lot of sense and they are far more likely to grow up obedient if they are heard.

Lack of submission affects our church life and ministry too. Everyone has an opinion, a desire, an idea, - two hundred people in church, - two hundred different voices! Leaders aren't always right, this is for sure, but they are leaders, with God's hand of protection and blessing on them. Remember David and Saul (1 Samuel 24:5 6). In spite of Saul's very obvious mistakes, David's heart remained submissive, not only to God but also to God's leaders. David understood that God deals with sinful leaders in His time. In church life, we need to have this deep confidence; that ultimately we are not in the hands of our leaders but in the hand of our God. God is the one who will release us, promote us and bless us, sometimes through our leaders, but if necessary, in spite of them.

I know that as church leaders we want a congregation who will back us 100%. Who, like Jonathan's armour bearer, will say, "Go ahead, do what is in your heart, we are with you all the way."(1 Samuel 14:7) Very few churches vote on issues anymore, yet it is a wise leader who will listen to his people, talk to them, keep them informed, be vulnerable and submissive to God before them, because only as we leaders genuinely submit to God, will we have true authority.

"Who, being in very nature God…Jesus…made Himself nothing, taking the very nature of a servant,…..He humbled Himself and became obedient to death…… Therefore God exalted Him to the highest place and gave Him a name that is above every name." Philippians 2:6-7

Chapter 38
Submission In Marriage

Submission is a big subject and, especially in this day and age, at times difficult.

I started the last chapter with a quote from an airline executive, which ended with, "no one wants to be thought of as a servant."

This chapter's quote shows us how different kingdom values are and is from Mark 10:43, said by Jesus Himself, "Whoever wants to be great, must become a servant", so simple to say, so hard to do.

Submission is at times simple and straightforward and at other times downright hard. We usually don't mind submitting to God, we know He is perfect, has our best interest at heart and knows the end from the beginning. But what about the imperfect church leader, that foul-mouthed boss, that controlling husband, that ungodly government? Not so easy - eh? Yet the Bible tells us to submit even under these circumstances, for Christ's sake, knowing He will bless us and promote us, that it will enhance our testimony and mature us.

But I didn't want to end this subject without being real and sincere and opening my heart on this subject, especially in the area of marriage. (I personally hate it when people speak or write in an idealistic, theoretical way without revealing struggles and heartaches, the apostle Paul certainly wasn't guilty of this.)

I am an open, talkative, humorous woman with an opinion on almost everything, (although I do realise mine isn't the only opinion or even the most important!) I am married to a lovely, godly, reserved man, who by and large prefers books to people and holds really strong opinions on only a few, usually spiritual subjects. He really doesn't mind what colour we paint the house, where we go on holiday, the state of the royal family or the rising crime in our nation. Unfortunately, I do!

Through the years, especially in my 30's and 40's, I struggled with submission. The struggle was not before my easy-going husband or even before my God, but before others, who I believed judged me as being unsubmissive. I struggled with my character. I chided myself; I should be meeker, quieter, and less opinionated. I was bewildered as I looked at the 'submit' scriptures. I was a serious Christian and I wanted to be the woman and wife God wanted me to be.

I write this article for all women like me, who have ever struggled with their God-given personality and wondered, "Am I submissive enough, do I please God?" - for all women who have ever been riddled with guilt and yet have so wanted to be a woman of God.

As a young Christian girl, a very dear male friend gave me a concordance. In the flyleaf, he wrote Proverbs 31:30 "Charm is deceptive and beauty is fleeting but the woman who fears the Lord is to be praised". As I sought God for a way ahead, this chapter became not only my guidance but also my reassurance. Here is the exemplary wife, a virtuous woman. Yet she is strong, intelligent, humorous, industrious, capable, godly and kind, a woman who looks after her house, her husband and her children well. She is wise and has understanding. She is good with money and buys and sells at profit. She also has a spiritual ministry. Her children love her and know they have a good mother.

And her husband? He praises her, he knows what a gem he has found. Her attitude and gifting bring him respect among the city elders. He is so confident in her, he knows he can trust her to run the affairs of his home and she will do it well. He therefore feels no need to control her. I am happy, relaxed and more than willing to take this woman as my role model. She is who I aspire to be.

I counsel you dear striving wife, talk to your husband. Not in a hurry or in front of the children, but at some lovely intimate time when you can voice your fears, your desires and aspirations to be the woman, God and he want you to be. Read Proverbs 31 together and reassure him she is your aim, to love him, care for him and respect him. To genuinely be his helpmeet, to raise your children together in a godly home and to release him to be the man God intended.

1 Peter 3:5 (The Message) "Cultivate inner beauty, the gentle, gracious kind that God delights in. The holy women of old were beautiful before God that way and were good, loyal wives to their husbands. Sarah for instance, taking care of Abraham, would address him as "my dear husband". You'll be true daughters of Sarah if you do the same, anxious and unintimidated."

Let us not allow the enemy to accuse, cause guilt, anxiety or intimidation. Dear sister as we obey God, we truly have nothing to fear.

SECTION 8

We Are A Chosen People

Chapter 39
We Are A Chosen People

In our late 30's, David and I found ourselves leading the only Pentecostal Evangelical church, at that time, on the Rock of Gibraltar. It was hard work but we loved it, the people were passionate and quick-tempered but that also made them enthusiastic and spontaneous, we loved them. The weather also totally suited us, months of Mediterranean sunshine every year, so although there were many other drawbacks, we loved our life. The church contained many ex-drug addicts and ex-alcoholics who had absolutely tremendous life-changing testimonies. We had open airs every week and baptised in water publicly in the sea and at these times, testimonies, of how Jesus had radically changed lives, held the crowd's attention. Strangely I found myself becoming envious of these "gutter to God" experiences, where was my story, what did I have to share? It was as this attitude was creeping into my heart, that in a wonderful revelation, God showed me how very special my personal testimony really was. Using Ephesians 1:4 God reinforced His calling and destiny in my life. He showed me I really was chosen.

"Long ago, even before he made the world, God loved us and chose us in Christ to be holy and without fault in his eyes."

God gave me a distinct picture of me as a blonde, 8-year-old little girl and through the ages, before even the earth was formed, I saw God's hand stretched out towards me, He laid His finger on me and said, "This child is mine". God then showed me how extraordinary my testimony really was. I was from a good, but as far as I knew at that time, totally non-believing home. No one was praying for me, no one was encouraging me to church, no-one spoke to me of the things of God and yet at the tender age of 8 years, I began to sense God calling me. I became preoccupied with God, who was He, where was He, could I know Him, did He know me? Round and round in my head, these questions and desires went. I looked everywhere I could think He might be found. I tried to read my mother's Sunday school prize Bible but although I could read well enough, I couldn't understand. I bought a rosary in Woolworths understanding that this had something to do with God. I attended any church indiscriminately, Methodist, Anglican, Roman Catholic, where was God? This quest continued more or less for 3 years. At one point a young Anglican curate told our Sunday school class that we could have a relationship with God, but he neglected to tell us how, otherwise I may have ended up Anglican, which of course, would have been no bad thing! Around about this time a young school friend invited me to a girls meeting in an Assemblies of God Pentecostal church, it was called Happy Hour for Girls and was run by 2 spinsters. I thought they were old at the time, but I expect now they were only in their late 30's. There, for the first time in my young life I heard, I could know God. I heard I was a sinner and I knew this was true, although by today's standards I was very innocent, I sometimes stole, mostly fruit, which I now find very sad, such things were a great luxury for a postwar child. But I also swore and lied and I knew that my parents would certainly not have approved, let alone Almighty God, so I knew this was the truth. I was indeed a sinner. But probably more importantly I heard that Jesus loved me, and came to earth and died to take the punishment for all my wrongdoing, and if I only believed in Him and asked Him into my heart, I could be "saved", another new word, and have the relationship with God I so craved. I asked Jesus to forgive me and to come into my life, but I must tell the truth and say my life didn't change at all. I was the same person but I continued to go to my little meeting.

Three years later, I had to leave Happy Hour and move up to the Youth meeting, I didn't mind, I'd made lots of lovely friends and together we grew up and went to Youth, although we are scattered all over the earth, we are still friends to this day. My spiritual experiences began to grow and I began to attend the Sunday meetings and it was one Sunday evening, sat on the back row, that I had my first real encounter with God! I don't remember the word but I remember the appeal. Did we want to be filled with the Holy Spirit? Well, I did, but courage wasn't a strong feature in my life at that point and I daren't go out to the front, but nevertheless, in my seat, I began to ask God for his Holy Spirit. Although I didn't speak in tongues or have any other external evidence, I distinctly felt God touch my life and I had on overwhelming desire to give my life 100% to Him. I can remember my thoughts to this day. "If God is real, I'd better stop playing around and give Him everything," and so I did. My life changed dramatically, I was 14 years old, I was a Christian and I loved Jesus, passionately! I tried to tell the whole world! My parents worried about me and my school friends tried to get a ban put on me to prevent me from singing choruses in class! Fortunately, my form teacher was a Brethren Christian who just tore their petition up with a smile! So my walk with Jesus began.

It is so important for us each to understand that whenever in our life we turn to Jesus, our salvation and our testimony are incredibly special.

"We are indeed a chosen people, a royal priesthood, a holy nation, a people belonging to God, that we may declare the praises of him who called us out of darkness into his wonderful light." 1 Peter 2:9

But finding Jesus so early in my life, would I be able to sustain this first love, this passion is the question I ask myself?

My biggest fear at this time in my life was that I would backslide, that I would change my mind and walk away from God. A wise fear, 1Corinthians 10:12 says, "So if you think you are standing firm, be careful that you don't fall."

In John 17:15 Jesus also prays in a similar way for His disciples then and now, that we would be protected. I used to pray and plead with God to keep me; I wanted to follow Him always. There was also pressure from my family who considered my conversion fanaticism. Now I am older and have parented children, I do understand their fears. But I think that being a Christian was actually part of my teenage rebellion. The more my family ridiculed me, the more I clung to Jesus. Now in my mid-seventies, that phase that my parents hoped

I was simply going through has lasted a very long time. God did answer mine and Jesus' prayers and kept me, only twice have I nearly backslidden, once over a minor church misunderstanding, which I thank God I had the sense, even at fifteen years, to wait and talk over with my Pastor. The second time, when I was about seventeen years old and a desire for the things of the world had begun to creep into my life, at this point, God brought David into my life and I was kept in the Kingdom.

Chapter 40
Maintaining Passion

In the last chapter, I shared with you my personal testimony of coming to Jesus and how God reinforced in my life that I was special and chosen by Him. And although my life had changed less dramatically than those who may have been older and who had therefore been touched more by the world and sin, my salvation was no less extraordinary and miraculous. Whether we come to Jesus when we are 9 years old, young and relatively innocent or 90 years old with a colourful past, we need to understand deep in our hearts, we have been marvelously and wonderfully saved.

But Jesus said the first and greatest commandment was that we should "Love the Lord our God with all our heart and with all our soul and with all our mind." (Matthew 22:37) that we should love God with passion.

If you have been a Christian for any length of time, you will understand, no matter how wonderful your testimony, how difficult it can sometimes be to remember why we came to be in this relationship with Jesus in the first place. It can be so easy to lose our "Mary" mentality of wanting nothing more in life than to sit at Jesus' feet, to be close to Him, to hear His voice and know His touch on our lives. Unwittingly our "Martha" side takes over, simply because in the Kingdom, in church life, there is so much to do and after all, we reason, someone has to do it. Without ever wanting it to happen, we can begin to lose our first love and our passion for Jesus Himself.

It can be compared to falling in love and marrying. I remember so easily what it felt like to be totally in love with my husband, when His touch thrilled me and I asked for nothing more than to be with him. But as the years roll on, life gets in the way, chores and responsibilities take over. How quickly, if we allow, it can diminish that love relationship and we begin to take each other for granted. Of course, serving is important but remember in spiritual life as in marriage, there is more to love than just service.

Being in love is so precious and we all believe it will last, but if we don't nurture it, feed it, protect it and give time for intimacy, all we will have are memories.

And our love relationship with Jesus is very similar; one of the church's names is the Bride of Christ. Yet it is so easy to forget why we first loved Him, to forget how He turned our life around. The buzz and excitement of our first love can diminish; we can reach a place where we no longer want to tell the whole world how wonderful He is. The responsibilities of ministry, worries and discouragement, if not checked, can crowd out passion. I remember, as a young teenage Christian, crying before God and asking Him to keep me, to never let me go, I wanted to love Him all my life. Even at that age, I had seen so many who had once walked with Jesus and known that love and yet had walked away. I understood very early in my spiritual life the scripture that says "If you think you are standing firm, be careful that you don't fall." (1 Corinthians 10:12) I was aware that falling was a possibility.

Down the years, so many times, I have experienced God answer that prayer. Every time my love has faltered, grown cool or passionless when duty and the world has crowded in, He has reminded me time and time again and in so many ways 'Remember your first love.' And true to His word, when I have been faithless, He has been so faithful, and drawn me back to Himself. Especially when ministry has seemed hard and discouraging, that still small voice has whispered, "Keep your eyes on me, this is not about service, this is about our love."

It is a wonderful privilege to serve God, to minister, to use our God-given gifting for His kingdom, but Jesus said, 'I have not called you servants, I have called you friends'. A man doesn't marry a wife to have his house cleaned, so God's heart is not that we will only serve Him, but that we will love Him in an everlasting increasingly intimate relationship.

Jesus said to Martha, "One thing only is essential, and Mary has chosen it". Let us make that same choice too.

SECTION 9

Forgiveness

Chapter 41
Forgiveness Part 1

Unfortunately, there are some things in the Christian faith which are imperatives. We must do them; there is no room for choice, negotiation or compromise. One of these is the command to forgive. If we are to take the Bible seriously, which of course we should, it is extremely dangerous for us not to forgive.

"When you stand praying, forgive so you will be forgiven." Mark 11:25

"Forgive or your heavenly Father will not forgive you." Matthew 6:14-15

Strong words indeed.

God doesn't just tell us to forgive so the other person is released from our animosity but because forgiveness is good for us. Forgiveness releases Kingdom power in our lives. It keeps us in relationship with God and with others. It keeps us healthy, body, soul and spirit. Unforgiveness, like stress, contributes to ill health. Forgiveness keeps us beautiful! I once knew a woman who had made unforgiveness a way of life. The most minor mistake or oversight would result in her bearing you a grudge. Unforgiveness was etched in her sad face.

I think, by now, all of us have come to understand that forgiveness is not something one feels, but something one chooses to do, because it is right, godly and good for me. As I go through the motions and actions of demonstrating forgiveness, my feelings catch up and, please God, we eventually know the blessing of forgetfulness. We choose not to remember. Forgiveness may even begin by simply wanting to forgive, or even wanting to want to let it go! But I want to share with you some other thoughts on the art and power of forgiveness.

Firstly, having worked and prayed our way to a place of forgiveness, do everything in your power not to rehearse the incident again. Some years ago, having been through a difficult period in ministry, we made a conscious and determined effort to forgive, bless, release and move on. We even wrote letters of reconciliation, release and regret for any part we may have played in the difficulty. But afterwards on several occasions, often for good reason, say to empathise with others, I would repeat the incident. Each time the old pain, hurt and rejection would return and I would have to struggle with feelings of unforgiveness all over again. Until God showed me, let it lie, it is in the past, dealt with, leave it in my hands and move on. It is like reopening an old but healing wound when we purposely recall our pain.

Secondly, to forgive does not mean it doesn't matter. It doesn't mean the other person wasn't wrong, it simply means, I leave it to God. "Vengeance is mine, I will repay, says the Lord." Romans 12:19

In about 1988, when we returned to U.K. God gave David and I an important scripture for that period in our lives, Isaiah 41.8-20. If an enemy rises up against us and our ultimate enemy, Satan, often uses other people, we know our God will be our protection, He is indeed for us.

This may sound arrogant and elitist, and I don't mean to be, but during a certain period, we saw God remove our enemies, definitely and firmly from us, as God protected us in the place He had called us. We almost wanted to say to our oppressors, 'Please be careful, God has promised us His protection.'

Thirdly, I do not believe to forgive necessarily means to put oneself in the place for further abuse. Some people are best forgiven and a distance made between us, especially when they refuse to see any fault on their part, or if the abuse is serious. Sometimes it is better to prune so-called friends who, physically, emotionally or spiritually, continually abuse us. Occasionally we may even have to protect others from that abuse.

Do you remember when Pope John Paul was stabbed? He forgave, but the man was still arrested, prosecuted and imprisoned for the protection of others. There is often a case to turn the other cheek, especially in minor misunderstandings, but not always, be wise and prayerful.

Fourthly be real. My husband does not find forgiveness difficult, that is a blessing, but neither is he the most sensitive of men. You may have tears in your eyes and he will not always realise you are hurting. That is not a blessing! Conversely, I am very sensitive to other people's pain and feel deeply for them, but on the negative side, I am easily hurt and take time to forgive. Forgiveness is something I have to work at.

Know your character, be real, talk over the pain and rejection with God. Tell Him how you feel, express the hurt, but then move on, allowing God to comfort you, heal you and show you the way ahead.

In the account of the crucifixion, as Jesus, "the Darling of Heaven", was being nailed to the cross by coarse, violent, rough soldiers, even while they drove the nails through His hands and feet, He said those powerful words, "Father forgive them, for they don't know what they are doing." So often, for even minor misdemeanours, the most spiritual of us need time to forgive and put it behind us, yet while the abuse was in full flow, Jesus forgave.

And the one who knows my darkest thoughts, my most impure motives, my struggle to love, my disobedience, selfishness and rebellion, not only loves me but also forgives me.

Experiencing such forgiveness, let us, therefore, forgive one another as he has graciously forgiven us.

Chapter 42
Forgiveness Part 2

When we are trying to walk in obedience to God and forgive, there are three people who I have found we struggle with the most.

When Jarrod was in Bible School, during one of the ministry times involving forgiveness, forgiving parents was highlighted. Jarrod said that most in the class went forward for prayer and he was one of only a few who felt had nothing to forgive. My first reaction was sorrow that so many felt pain from their parenting. But my second reaction was gratitude that Jarrod saw us as reasonable parents because obviously, we had not been perfect.

Perhaps I should just confess here, I do get a certain amount of "blame" from both my sons for not breastfeeding them. They claim if I had, they would have been taller and wouldn't have allergies. I tell them, all I can do is apologise and ask them to forgive me!

But I think this is my point. Parenting is a difficult and demanding job, for which we receive no training. It is very easy to blame our upbringing and therefore our parents for all our problems, hang-ups and weaknesses. While I understand there are neglectful and abusive parents, for the vast majority of us, our parents did the best they could with the wisdom they had. If I dig too much around my own childhood and relationship with my parents, there is pain. In those days parents didn't understand how important it was to praise, encourage, affirm and express love to their children. But I long ago understood, my parents did the best they knew how. When I was tiny and vulnerable, they sheltered me, fed me, nursed me through serious childhood illnesses, protected me from harm and taught me right from wrong, for which I will always be deeply grateful. And even if you discovered that your parents never really wanted you or planned you, know this, God did. It makes me chuckle to know God wanted us so much; He overrode the plans of a man and a woman. Did they want a boy? God wanted a girl, or of course vice versa. In Him you are planned, wanted, chosen and accepted. (Psalm 139:13-17) Very often we need to become parents ourselves before we truly understand and are able to forgive our own parents.

The other person we often struggle to forgive is God. Not because He has done anything wrong, but because He didn't answer prayer in the way we want. Do you, like me, ever tell God how it would be best to answer prayer? - Advise Him what would be the greatest spiritual influence? "Lord if you did A, B, C and D, so many would be blessed and brought to you and your name would be glorified." Unfortunately, God doesn't always agree with me.

I remember some years ago praying for a young man in his early 30's who had a brain tumour. His wedding was one of our first in Hull and we were especially fond of him and his wife. Many people fasted and prayed for his healing, but he died. I was very angry with God and I kicked against this untimely death.

I reasoned with God, "Of all the nerds in this world, of all the child molesters, women beaters and generally pretty rotten men, you take this handsome, spiritual, loving husband and father, Lord he was even planning to enter the ministry. What a testimony his healing would have been."

When these things happen in our lives, they shake us to the core, don't they? Why did God say no or take them? Was there a purpose? Did we not pray enough, fast enough, have enough faith? Anger, disappointment and guilt are directed at God.

I have a great need for sincerity, reality and integrity in relationships and have found to express these feelings to God is the way through. I know I have a God who does not fail, who loves me and those I have been praying for more than I could ever comprehend. Although in this life I may never have an answer, He does and ultimately I trust

Him. Do you remember in John 6:66, where many left following Jesus because they didn't like what He said? When He asked the disciples "Will you leave me too?" Their answer should be our answer when we don't understand, "Where will we go Lord, you have the words of eternal life."

And finally, we need to learn to forgive ourselves. The Bible tells us that the devil is the accuser of the brethren. He regularly seeks to accuse me, reminding me of mistakes and weaknesses even of my youth almost half a century ago. Things I have acknowledged before God, things I have put right, learned from and grown, yet he digs them up, holds them before me and accuses. All we need do at these times is declare the word of God over our lives and before our enemy.

"If we confess our sins, he is faithful and just and will forgive us our sins and purify us from all unrighteousness." 1 John 1:9 Therefore, enemy, I am forgiven!

Chapter 43
Forgiveness Part 3

Thankfully, for the vast majority of us, forgiveness involves fairly minor incidents. At the time they may feel extremely painful and cause us sleepless nights and tears, but time is a great healer and when we look back in hindsight, we realise the event only made us stronger. But what about when someone potentially destroys our life, when the pain is so huge and grotesque we can never imagine recovering. What about when they are not sorry or will not acknowledge their fault? What about when the very one who should love us, nurture us and protect us, seeks to use us and destroy us? What about when our loved ones are hurt? Can we as Christians forgive the unforgivable?

Some years ago, I clicked on the T.V. during the day and got one of the better American chat shows. The guest was a woman whose mother and little daughter had been killed by a female drunk driver. She said when she received this news she heard the primeval scream of a wounded animal. It was her own voice. It totally devastated her life. The drunk driver was put in prison, but as the months rolled by, this woman, who was a Christian, began to feel compassion for the offender and the guilt she must be feeling at her crime. Months later still, God prompted her to write to the offender still in prison. They began to correspond and eventually met. The driver of the car said she was terrified to meet the woman whose life she had so carelessly destroyed. But as they met, the Christian opened her arms to the other woman and assured her, "I forgive you." This woman was so touched by this gracious, forgiving attitude, she too became a Christian and God turned her life around. The chat show host asked how such forgiveness was possible, it was not understandable. The answer was, "Only with the help of Jesus." The host with amazement on her face declared, "You persuade all of us to believe!"

There are some of us who have been abused, perhaps even sexually, how do we forgive, reclaim our lives and move on? Because forgive we must, if we are not to allow our abuser not only to harm us, but also to rob us of our whole lives, limiting our spiritual growth. Please God, let a strength from you rise up in us, that declares, "I am not a victim, and abuser, you will not steal my life." Don't think for one minute that I am seeking to trivialise the effect of this sort of abuse. Like many young women, I was subject to sexual harassment, but on one occasion, I was mildly sexually assaulted. The mixture of emotions this brought up in my life was bewildering, everything from fear to anger and even guilt, yes, I know - weird, but I worried my appearance had encouraged it. More than 30 years later, I cannot walk down a country lane and hear bicycle wheels behind me, without my heart beating faster and calling on Jesus for protection. This was the most minor of assaults, but if that could cause such long-term distress, I can barely imagine the pain involved in serious abuse.

Don't forget in a previous chapter I mentioned that to forgive does not mean they were not in the wrong. Their actions may even have been criminal and others may actually have to be protected from them. I also mentioned to forgive does not mean to put oneself in the same place to be hurt again. To forgive is to release the hurt, the pain, the suffering to God and to know He will deal with it. 'It is mine to avenge, I will repay says the Lord.'

Please understand, unforgiveness does not punish our abuser; what it actually does is continue to harm us.

Hard as it is to accept this or even to say it, I still believe God can take the most horrendous pain in our lives, turn it around and use it, not only to bless, mature and shape our lives, but so that we might bless and inspire others to receive their healing too.

I love the Old Testament story of Joseph and use it a lot in ministry. Joseph undoubtedly knew what it was to be hated, rejected, abused, lied about and forgotten; time and time again, yet remained tenderhearted. And when God at last brought him to his promised position, he was able to forgive his abusers and say, "You meant it for harm, but God meant it for good." And as his life moved forward, he called his children "Manasseh", meaning forgetfulness, and "Ephraim", meaning double fruitfulness or blessing. God caused him to forget his incredibly painful past and to move forward into a place of double blessing. Remember God says to us, "I will restore the years the locust has eaten." That stolen time will be given back to us. (The story of Joseph is found in Genesis 37-50)

Whatever the pain of our past, God help us to forgive, God bless us with forgetfulness and doubly bless us and make us fruitful as we move forward with Him.

SECTION 10

Being An Influence

Chapter 44
My City, Kingston-Upon-Hull

I wonder, in what sort of a city, town or village God has placed you, either by birth or by adoption?

Nineteen years ago, in 1988, our family returned from 10 years living in Gibraltar, on the tip of Spain and at the mouth of the Mediterranean. Having spent so many years in a land of Latin temperament and among a people with a great sense of personal pride and self-esteem, God brought us to work in this City called Hull. Hull is a north-eastern city of about 250,000 people, nearer to 400,000 if you count the surrounding villages, with, especially at that time, a serious problem with self – worth.

Nineteen years ago, I could only find one coffee shop that made cappuccinos, - a serious shortcoming after the café culture of Gibraltar. The first time I asked one of our women to join me for a coffee, she asked: "What for, - couldn't we make one at home?"

Hull's self-worth had suffered greatly after the virtual closure of the fishing industry, which had given it a sense of identity, wealth and purpose in the past. Areas of the City were run down and large neglected council estates were failing to meet the social needs of the people.

To further grind their noses into their lack of status, Hull was top of every national negative list and bottom of every positive one. We even featured as number one in the book – "Crap Towns: The 50 Worst Places to Live in the UK", (Sorry about the 'C' word, but that's the title.)

It quotes a former resident as saying it's "a sad place of unemployment, teenage pregnancy, heroin addiction, crime, violence, and rampant self-neglect".

It is hard for people to hold their heads high under such unrelenting criticism, and, unfortunately, there was truth in many of the negative comments.

When God brings you to a City such as ours, what can you do? How can we, as His people, help to turn the situation around?

A few years ago an international speaker and his team held a conference in our City. Because the meetings weren't well attended, the City yet again came under sharp criticism for its apparent lukewarmness and apathy.

The minister spoke to us about attitudes in Hull and we shared with him how we felt about this place where God had called us.

First of all, we said, the City is not Hull, but Kingston-upon-Hull. Hull is simply a little river that runs through our centre. Kingston, of course, means Kings Town and we shared how we regularly declare our City to be the Town, not only of the King, but of the King of Kings. What's in a name? – Perhaps little, but possibly a lot.

Secondly, we acknowledge that our City, like so many other British Cities, has problems and through the years, we as a church have regularly and fervently prayed. As a congregation, we bless the City with extended hands and declare over it every positive attribute God brings to mind. We bless her with live churches, jobs and prosperity, good schools with godly staff, we bless our police and our prisons, we ask wisdom for our councils and we bless families and homes. Through the years we have regularly and purposefully prayer walked her streets.

Thirdly, we told this visiting minister, we encourage each other never to criticise the City, but to bless her and hold up Hull and her people daily before God. Together we remember the positive words of prophecy spoken down the years by a succession of godly men and women. We declare out loud these words to encourage and remind ourselves that "God loves Kingston-upon-Hull and has kingdom purposes for her."

Jeremiah exhorts us to pray for the peace and prosperity of the city to which God has taken us, for when it prospers, we, too, will prosper. (Jeremiah 29:7)

When God brings us to a city, town or village to serve Him, it is in our interest to love and bless that place and her people. It is godly to overlook weaknesses and to remember strengths. To only see the negative, whether in a person, a church, or a place is a ploy of the enemy, and to be resisted at all costs.

Kingston-upon-Hull today is a far different City, still with many weaknesses to pray about, but with many strengths for which we thank God and rejoice together, as a church, at every step forward and every victory. (This year 2017 we are the City of Culture!)

We now have many new restaurants and coffee shops, - (apparently a sign of growing wealth!) We have two huge new Shopping Malls, one built on stilts over the waters of a quay. We have a stunning Submarium on the banks of the river Humber and a big new Football Stadium. We have a beautiful continental style Marina right in the City and many neglected areas are being regenerated.

Hull is also a busy commercial seaport with daily car and passenger ferries to Europe, not to mention our historic old town with its art galleries and museums, and of course, the beautiful and iconic Humber Bridge.

This year we are incredibly proud as a Church and as a City to celebrate the 200th. anniversary of the Abolition of the Slave Trade, the life work of Christian M.P. for Hull, William Wilberforce, also born and educated in this City

So whether the City in which God has placed you is elegant, prosperous and cultured, or like our City, with still some way to go, - declare over her, as we do, -

Kingston-upon-Hull, You are the Top and not the Bottom, the Head and not the Tail! (From the scripture in Deuteronomy 28:13 "The LORD will make you the head, not the tail. You will always be at the top, never at the bottom.")

Chapter 45
"Do Not Oppress Foreigners In Any Way"
Exodus 22.21 NLT

Written at least a decade ago, how pertinent and relevant this chapter remains…

For a long time, I have wanted to write this article, but I have always sensed it would be highly controversial, with extremely wide and strongly held opinions.

But the other day, after reading several negative articles in the newspapers and then, as I crossed the city, overhearing negative comments between two middle-aged women, I decided the time was right.

I want to write about the foreigners within our shores.

Like many of you, I am incensed when I read that crime in some areas has risen by 35% and chief police officers attribute it to immigrants.

I am deeply troubled to hear that so many now live on U.K. benefits, even receiving Family Allowance or credit for children still residing in their own country, when our own pensioners, who have contributed taxes all their lives, receive so little.

I am angered by people of other faiths, inciting violence and terrorism on one hand, whilst seeking asylum from their own troubled, corrupt and oppressive nations on the other.

I am saddened to know that amongst Oxford's Christian spires, the Islamic call to pray three times a day may soon be heard.

And probably, most disturbing of all is the understanding that because of the world in which we live, in which political correctness rules, none of us dare speak out for fear of being labeled racist. Our government is afraid to enforce boundaries, to the detriment of our own people.

There is no doubt that the media fuels these feelings of fear and helplessness and I have made a conscious decision to limit how much I read.

Above all else, I choose to be a woman of God. My personal opinion is immaterial. When I became a Christian, Jesus and His word began to shape who I am, how I behave and what I believe. I refuse to let the tabloid press form my opinions. And who of us could say, hand on heart, that if we had been born in a violent, impoverished and corrupt nation, we wouldn't have sought better for ourselves and our children?

The Bible has much to say about the foreigner and the stranger within our land.

Leviticus 19:33 " When an alien lives with you in your land, do not mistreat him…. treat him as one of your native-born…. Love him as yourself."

Hebrews 13:2 " Do not forget to entertain strangers, for by so doing some people have entertained angels without knowing it."

See also Matt 25:35-40

And more than that, I love living in a nation with such diversity. I would hate to live in an all white, all English speaking country. I love the national costumes, the foreign languages, the exciting food, and the stunningly beautiful different skin colours. One of my favourite coffee shops is always half full of foreign students and asylum seekers, laughing and talking animatedly and drinking their espressos.

Our church is enriched and enlivened by Christians from nations all over the world. They are instrumental in our recent growth; they influence our prayer and our worship. They are men and women of God, who we deeply respect. They are educated, work hard and raise their children with strong moral principles. I would not want a life that did not include them.

I am proud to belong to a nation that shelters the oppressed but I would urge our government to put in place and enforce immigration laws for all our sakes, including the immigrant. And if I could, I would write a letter to every foreigner entering our nation, that says something like this: -

"Dear Immigrant/Asylum seeker/foreigner,

Welcome to this great and ancient land. We pray that while you are with us, our God will bless and prosper you and your loved ones. We pray that you will live in safety, have a good life and make many new friends. But for you to make the most of this experience, please try to learn a little of our language to help you to communicate with us.

And when our eyes meet, please smile back at me, because I genuinely wish you well and a smile transcends all languages.

Work hard and contribute to this nation that has given you shelter, and should you fall on hard times, make use of our welfare state until you are back on your feet. And "until" is a keyword. Most of us despise even our own people who see benefits as a chosen way of life.

Don't contribute to our crime, violence, immorality and vice, we have enough of it already, it is destroying us. Instead bring your strong morals, family values and a desire to live better lives.

Practice your own faith, without fear and in safety. You should know many of us respect you for your firmly held beliefs.

And when you look at Great Britain, you may see it as a secular society and there is now some truth in that, but you will find that at our heart and shaping much of our greatness is our God and His Son, Jesus Christ. Still today, in our nation, millions continue to be

His ardent followers. And our prayer is that this Jesus, our God will bless you and reveal Himself to you, because to know Him will bring the biggest life change of all, because He says, "I am come that they may have life, and have it to the full." John 10:10

Chapter 46
Ambassador For Christ

When I first became a Christian almost half a century ago, one of the principles of godly living, which I quickly grasped, was the divine calling to "Go into all the world and preach the good news". This can undoubtedly be attributed to the fact that I was saved in a church with a strong evangelical ethos. And in seeking to fulfil this important commission, I bought myself a little badge which declared importantly "Ambassador for Christ". (2 Corinthians 5:20) I proudly wore this statement on my lapel constantly, changing it from coat to sweater, from school uniform to casual wear, much to my mother's consternation and cries of "you'll ruin your clothes!" This little badge brought many opportunities to speak about Jesus, wherever I was.

In the world, an Ambassador lives in a foreign country, while representing another, his own. And this is exactly what God has called us to do, isn't it? Yes, we live on Earth, but we are actually citizens of heaven and as such represent that kingdom and that King.

Ambassadors may live in a culture totally foreign to their own. And this can certainly be said of us. Romans 1:26-32 paints an accurate, but a distressing picture of the world in which we live today, homosexuality, wickedness, strife, gossips, God-haters etc.

Yet God calls us to represent His kingdom, a kingdom of righteousness, godliness, unselfishness, purity, love and service.

Structured evangelism is excellent and great training. Such activities as street work; doorbell and open airs both sow seed and produce fruit. But these are generally, even among the most enthusiastic, only for a few hours each week.

As "Ambassadors for Christ" we are never off duty, it is our essence, who we are. Doing the garden, we are an "Ambassador for Christ", in work, we are an "Ambassador for Christ" – in the gym, the coffee shop, college, school, the supermarket, we are "Ambassadors for Christ" and as such, I believe we are being watched.

I cannot tell you how many times David and I have been approached, or have later been told we have been seen by, to us, complete strangers, sometimes even in another City. Just the other day, having a coffee in the sun, a young man approached us and asked if David was the minister of New Life Church. We had never met him before, but he had been at a funeral that David had conducted, and he said how much the service had touched him.

I'm reading a Dave Gilpin book at the moment and he says "Your influence goes far beyond what you could ever imagine," and just a few months ago I had proof of this.

I received an email from a young man in his forties. He had found us on our website. He asked if I remembered him and of course, I did. He was the son of a friend from more than thirty years ago. She was one of a few Christian women, from a couple of churches, who had a time of fellowship and prayer on Wednesday mornings in the village where we lived. He reminded me that one day he called by my home to collect his mother from one of those meetings, - he was ten years old. He told me in this email that my home had such an impact on him that the next day, in his school diary, he wrote - Yesterday I went to "the special house." The only physical and obvious sign in our house that we were Christians was a plaque that said "Christ is the head of this house, the unseen guest at every meal, the silent listener to every conversation."

A few years later, this young boy became a Christian, and when he now gives his testimony, he cites our home as one of the milestones that led him to God. How surprised, honoured and blest we felt! And we realised, what a responsibility.

We are being watched. People take note of who we are, how we react, how we live, our attitudes, and - if the recent email is anything to go by, - our home. I believe only in eternity will we know the lives we have touched while representing Jesus.

My oldest son, Jason, worked as an Aid worker in Afghanistan for a year, for a Christian agency. Of course, they could not openly witness, but he said it was obvious the Muslims watched them and their behaviour. Occasionally their observations and subsequent questions were amusing. Every morning before work, the staff all went into a small office to pray. Before entering, they would all remove their jackets and hang them outside. One Afghan asked if the removal of the jacket was a significant religious ritual! – (They apparently have to remove tobacco from their person before prayer.) – It led to a short time of speaking about the Christian faith.

We are indeed saved by grace and we only have to believe and have faith in Jesus to be saved. We cannot earn our salvation. But God give us faith and belief that changes the way we live and make us truly, in every area of our lives, every day, every moment – "Ambassadors for Christ"

Paul says in Acts 20:24 TLB. – "My life is worth nothing unless I use it for doing the work assigned me by the Lord Jesus."

We have the privilege and responsibility of being assigned to earth, to represent our King and His Kingdom.

Chapter 47
Joy

My concordance tells me, and I quote,

"In no other religion and in no other literature is joy so conspicuous as in Christianity and the Bible…Christianity stands firm so long as men who have it are invested with joy."

In other words, joy sets Christians apart from all other faiths.

I have loved preparing this article because it is who I aspire to be, a woman of joy, with, as the French say, a "Joie de vie".

Every single one of us, who call ourselves Christian and have Jesus in our lives, are entitled to and should exhibit joy. It is what Jesus came to bring. In the beginning, at His earthly birth, the Angels told the shepherds that they brought, "Good news of great JOY, for all people." (Luke 2:10)

As a man, during His years of ministry, Jesus reinforced this, "I have told you this, so that my JOY may be in you and that your JOY may be complete." (John 15:11)

Romans 14:17 paraphrased, says, "The Kingdom of heaven is not "laws" but righteousness, JOY and peace in the Holy Spirit."

And in Galatians 5:22 JOY is a fruit of the Spirit, which will automatically grow in the right circumstances.

The Old Testament is also full of JOY scriptures, my favourite being Nehemiah 8:10, "Do not mourn or weep or grieve, for the JOY of the Lord is your strength."

The Joy of the Lord is a source of great spiritual, physical and mental well-being, which everyone needs.

But although Joy is provided in abundance for each of us who knows Jesus, I have found it is, in practice, often in short supply.

"Joy is a flag flown high from the castle of my heart, for the King is in residence there." So goes the old children's action chorus, so why is our flag of Joy often at half-mast?

Probably because life often throws pebbles, rocks and even boulders into our fountain of Joy and if we allow this to build up, its free flow may become restricted.

Personal problems and difficulties can rob us of this Joy. Just this week one of our young men was mugged, robbed and his friends physically hurt. If we allow, such things can hinder not only our peace of mind but also our Joy.

Again there are many serious world issues that if we dwell on them and neglect to keep our eyes on our God, can also be another rock blocking our Joy.

Sin will rob us of our joy. King David after repenting of his sin, pleaded with God, "Restore to me the JOY of your salvation." (Psalm 51:12)

Striving to "keep up with the Joneses", materially and spiritually, will rob us of our Joy, 1 Timothy 6:6 says, "Godliness with contentment is great gain."

Yet Philippians 4:4 tells us to "Rejoice always," even when we are in need; keep rejoicing because we have a great God who meets those needs.

And Isaiah 54:1 says, "Sing barren woman, Shout for JOY," It's a command to counteract barrenness, dryness, emptiness and unfruitfulness, both in our natural and our spiritual lives.

What happens, I wonder? - Does the "Shout of Joy" dislodge the rocks that choke our spring? I believe this is true.

All of us have a tendency, at times, to lose our joy, and often a good talking to is all that's required.

King David says in Psalm 43:4-5, "To God my exceeding Joy," then contrarily, he goes on to chastise himself and say, "Why are you downcast O my soul, why so disturbed, hope in God."

I love the simplicity of this. When Joy seems in short supply, don't accept it. Let's give ourselves a good chastising. Anti-depressants are not needed 99.9% of the time, counselling not needed; but keeping God central in our vision 100% of the time, a necessity; He alone is our JOY Giver.

GRACE, in Greek, is Charis, from the same root as Chara meaning- JOY, and also from the same root as Chairo meaning- TO REJOICE. In other words, Grace, Joy and Rejoicing have the same source. It seems Joy is a by-product of His Grace. Therefore we, who know His Grace, should have His Joy and be a Rejoicing people.

Ephesians 1:3 says, "He has blessed us with every spiritual blessing." I am right with God, forgiven, guilt-free, unashamed, on my way to heaven and all unmerited and by His grace. His grace should indeed cause us to be full of joy.

Joy is also a testimony to the world around us. We are "Ambassadors for Christ", and we represent a King and a Kingdom of Joy. Yet so often this is not what the world sees and we are portrayed as miserable and dour. Dear Christian, don't let our joy be so deep that no – one ever sees it, let it reach our faces. If your face wants to smile, let it; if it doesn't - make it!

There is a lovely yoghurt advert that talks of "Licking the lid of life." This really ought to be us, sucking the juice out of life; enjoying every day God gives us on this earth. Joy keeps us well, beautiful and attractive to others. No one is drawn to God by a misery; the world has that in abundance.

The world in all its drugs, alcohol, promiscuity, materialism, etc., seeks joy. – Let them see that we have it. Joy is our advert that shows the world "Jesus touches parts that other faiths don't."

And even when life is incredibly tough and circumstances have thrown into our JOY, not a rock, not a boulder, but a huge concrete slab, let's remember, "Weeping may endure for a night, but JOY comes in the morning." Psalm 30:5

We have a God who deals with our pain and our sadness and replaces it with His Joy.

Psalm 30:11-12

"You have turned my wailing into dancing;

You removed my sackcloth and clothed me with JOY,

That my heart may sing to you and not be silent.

O LORD my God, I will give you thanks for forever!"

I wrote this article from the depths of my heart, but I in no way want to minimise the pain, distress and bereavement we human beings occasionally encounter. This article was written around the months following little Madeleine McCann's disappearance. When we see the torment in her parents' eyes, it is hard to believe they will ever experience real joy again. There is also a process we go through in bereavement or any extreme pain of loss and we should allow ourselves to travel through this process without guilt or pressure. We do need to be real and we are not always in happy circumstances, but joy is much deeper and more substantial than just happy. If I may be a little light-hearted for a minute, I am happy on a sunny day, sitting outside a coffee shop, enjoying a cappuccino with a group of friends. Joy is a much deeper experience not dependent on our surroundings or circumstances.

Habakkuk 3:17-18 talks of a time when everything in life is failing, but the writer's strong resolve is, "Yet I will rejoice in the Lord, I will be joyful in God my Saviour."

Chapter 48
Our Core Values

We live in a drastically changing world. In my lifetime, I have experienced changes in technology, medicine and the wealth of our nation. I consider these to be mostly positive, but unfortunately, some changes have been distinctly negative. Time will not stand still, no matter how much we might want this, and in the face of this change, "What manner of people ought we to be?" 2 Peter 3:11 What are our core values that will never change, no matter what happens in our world and the society in which we live?

When our Church went through a transition and senior leadership passed from one generation to the next, Jarrod brought us seven core values which, though much would undoubtedly change, these never would.

1. We Are A People Of The Word

The Bible, God's word is our yardstick, our plumbline and our guide. Prophecy, revelation, experience, emphasis, new values and even other core values, stem from this, - what does God's word say about this issue?

Matthew 24:35, "Heaven and earth will pass away, but not my words."

John 17:17, "Your word is truth."

In today's world, its moral standards may seem old-fashioned but Christians cannot have their own code of practice and prosper. The word of God has proved itself over centuries to be authentic, profitable, wise and still relevant in our modern society.

We may not always fully understand or even agree with God's word but we need to embrace, adhere to and stand on it. When talking with people who want to live differently to Gods standard, it's wonderfully releasing to be able to say, "Don't argue with me, this is not my opinion, this is God's word."

2. We Are A People Of Worship

Prayer, praise, worship, communication with God, relationship and not ritual set us apart as Christians. Being a religious and nominal Christian damages and weakens the Christian church. Worship turns mountains into molehills; worship draws God's presence; it breaks the power of the enemy; opens prison doors and appropriates answers to prayer and sometimes it takes sacrifice. One of the meanings of worship is "to kiss". What a wonderful, intimate picture of our relationship with our heavenly Father, that as we worship, we kiss Him.

3. We Are A People Of Faith

God's word says, "Without faith, it is impossible to please God." (Hebrews 11:6)

Hebrews 11:1 tells us, "Faith is being sure of what we hope for and certain of what we do not see."

And then encouragingly Ephesians 2:8, "We are saved by grace, through faith and this is a gift of God." The faith God tells us to have, He gives us and Romans 10:17 tells us this faith comes, "By hearing the Message."

Faith is a guilt area and the enemy constantly accuses us because he knows how powerful faith is. Remember, faith as small as a mustard seed moves mountains Matthew 17:20.

We are saved by faith, are Christians by trusting in and believing what we cannot touch or see but are persuaded by a God, whose influence, love and power affect every day of our lives.

4. We Are A People Of The Family

This is where the greatest change and the most blatant satanic attack results in the breakdown of western society. Divorce, fornication, adultery, homosexuality are rife in our nation and in the 21st century considered to be the norm.

There is also something fundamentally wrong with a society that has laws to prohibit the hunting of foxes and yet permits, even encourages, the tearing of human babies from their mother's wombs.

Let us declare to our world, God is for lifelong marriage and the family. Marriage, between a man and his wife, is the only place where sex is blessed and actively encouraged. Let us declare that children are a precious gift and reward from God and it is our sacred and holy duty to love, train and discipline them for Jesus.

5. We Are A People Of His Presence

Our aim is not excellent music, eloquent preaching, a strong social action team or even a united church; our goal is His presence in our lives and meetings. We host secular conferences in our venue and are asked, "What is this place, there is such an atmosphere here?" Or amusingly, "Can I live here, there is such a sense of peace?" God's presence defines us. The children of Israel, even in the wilderness, knew God's presence, day and night.

2 Chronicles 5:13-14 tells of a time when the presence of God was so heavy the priests could not minister. His presence changes lives and attitudes, bringing healing, salvation and ultimately revival.

6. We Are A People Of Power

Matthew 28:18 Jesus says, "All power is given to me."

Acts 1:8," You will receive power."

Why then is the church so often seen as weak, irrelevant and effeminate, when in truth our God still today, has the power to save, heal, deliver and bless and even more wonderfully, entrusts us with that same power. In fact, His word says we will do even greater things in His name! (John 14:12)

"God has not given us a spirit of fear, but of love, POWER and a sound mind." 2 Timothy 1:7

7. We Are A People Of Mission

The divine commission to "go into all the world and preach the gospel" has never been rescinded. It remains our divine calling to tell others of God's love. Romans 10:14 says, "How will they be saved unless we tell them". Our church's vision statement is "Carrying God's glory - from the neighbourhood to the nations." A hurting world needs to see God's power and glory and know He loves them. Our mission is to share Jesus.

Our unchanging God, in a changing world, says to people, "Will you come to me?"

Chapter 49
Speak Up

The Bible has much to say about the tongue, it's unruliness, it's power to bless or curse and if we have it under control, we are described as mature (James 3). Much of the time, keeping our words few is highly encouraged, something of a challenge for the chatterboxes amongst us, of whom I count myself. Certain holy orders take vows of silence, I would suspect among other reasons, to minimise sin. And while I understand the wisdom of "keeping our words few", more and more I believe we Christians have a God-given responsibility to speak up and speak out.

We are living in a generation in moral decline and it is no longer acceptable to lock ourselves in our churches in holy and blessed huddles and deplore what is happening outside. Even to pray for this lost generation is not sufficient, God has given us a voice and silence is not always golden.

So if you are a chatterbox, allow me to encourage you and say if used appropriately, it can be a God-given gift and tool. Use your voice to pray, to worship, to encourage others, to befriend, to communicate the gospel and to speak out about situations in our world that are immoral, ungodly, unbiblical, unethical and dangerous to our children.

Other faiths and minority groups are not shy to verbalise what offends them and are quick to demand the right to be heard, but in such matters, so many Christians lack conviction and courage. It may be we believe nothing will change, that our one voice is too small to be heard, but that's the enemies' tactic, isn't it? And this isn't correct. For example, I understand that for every one complaint made to television, it is estimated that approximately 10,000 other people will feel the same! This makes our one voice important and influential.

To speak out against an evil is not easy and most of us don't enjoy doing it. Even speaking to a brother in sin is challenging and not often immediately well received, no matter how gently and lovingly done, but in my experience, in time bears godly fruit.

To speak out against an evil in our world is similarly difficult and as well as courage takes skill and wisdom. A recent television programme followed fundamental Christians voicing protests over several issues. And while I thoroughly agree and applaud their protest, their manner was at times perturbing. The apparent belligerence, lack of humour and biblical knowledge portrayed us again as fanatics, irrelevant to this world and with little to back up our beliefs. Be careful; be aware of television and journalistic editing and the condemning sound-bite!

Over the years, like many of you, I have protested over several issues. Let's continue to sign any petition that comes our way to promote biblical standards in our nation, write letters of complaint and personally approach, whenever necessary, to appeal for a stronger moral stance. But God give us wisdom and skill in the manner and wording of our appeal.

For example, I only occasionally, as appropriate, mention I am a Christian or bring Jesus or the Bible into the discussion. I remain calm and polite but firm at all times. I bring as much positive encouragement as I can and only then say clearly why I am offended.

One fairly minor example, in our area we have a lovely little market town. On one visit, I noticed children's T-shirts bearing four- letter word slogans. I spoke to the stallholder on the inappropriateness of these garments, but my approach was totally rejected. I then persisted, went higher and wrote to the manager of the market. I praised the lovely town, said what an asset and attraction the beautiful market was and then voiced the cause of my complaint.

The manager's reply was warm, grateful and in agreement that such produce was inappropriate and the product was removed. One tiny victory in the scheme of things I know, but still a tiny victory for decency and dozens of vulnerable and impressionable children, in my area, are not wearing a vulgar shirt!

I appeal to our spiritual leaders, speak out on our behalf. Approach government and politicians and others in high places, encourage the good and speak out against evil. Bring a wise, measured, biblical, moral, fluent, gracious voice to the table, let the church once again bring guidance, direction and relevance to this nation. I honour John Sentamu, the Archbishop of York, for the strength and integrity he brings to our national church. He regularly speaks up and speaks out in both words and actions for Britishness, for Christianity and against moral and ethical decline both here in Britain and worldwide. I honour the Catholic Church for its strong stand against immorality and declining values. God gave us a voice, let's use it.

SECTION 11

Changes

Chapter 50
The Why And How Of Transition

In March 2005 David and I handed over Senior Leadership of New Life Church, Hull to our younger son, Jarrod. It was only the second church we had ever led, and we had been leading it for seventeen years. Our love, commitment and loyalty to the people of New Life and even to the City of Hull was tremendous, and yet for a few years, we had known the day was coming when we would wholeheartedly relinquish leadership.

Almost three years after the changeover, and feeling with all my heart this has been a successful transition, and seeing, hearing and knowing that so many aren't, this article evolved.

First of all - Why Transition?

Why hand on the baton, especially at a time of life when so many have said - "Why now, you have loads of life and ministry left in you!" – and of course we have.

We were, at that time, in our early sixties and very healthy. But we had seen large, successful, flourishing churches crumble when the leader had died or had simply begun to go downhill and lose their physical, mental and spiritual edge.

We had a minister colleague whose life had been dedicated to his church. Not seeing, or perhaps unwilling to see, that his health was deteriorating; he hung on until the congregation had to "encourage" him out of his leadership position. Although I am sure much healing has since gone on, he and his wife, at the time, were obviously devastated. Discerning and understanding timing is important for all of us, understanding when to relinquish even a successful and flourishing ministry is crucial, both for the ministry and all concerned.

Also, care for a people who have loved you and supported you has to be taken into consideration. New Life deserved "the best", and we didn't in any way, shape or form want to hold them back because of our need to hold on to them. Our desire, above our own situation, was that "His Kingdom would come" in New Life and our City, and this was our primary concern and if that involved more youthful, dynamic leadership, so be it.

Also, I believe it is unfair to hold back the next generation for too long. – Yes, they must mature, - Yes they must grow and they must prove themselves, - but don't let us hold them back until the fire, enthusiasm, youth and vision are driven out of them or diverted elsewhere. Let us harness it and allow the Kingdom of Heaven to benefit from such gifting.

And yes we still had loads to give, but in our hearts too, is a desire for new adventures, to go through some of those doors God is opening to us, there will be life and ministry after New Life! So having decided transition will happen, that the baton will be handed on, how can we prepare and plan for success.

Firstly, the younger man should be extremely well known to you and trusted. In our case, it is our son. We know him well, including his weaknesses. (Jarrod had been away to Bible School and had an itinerant ministry before leading New Life.) If not your physical son, at least a spiritual son, one you have raised, taught and nurtured in the church.

If you have to bring in a successor, I suggest you let them work as your associate for a few years. Jarrod worked for us casually for several years while being itinerant and then for one year formally as our associate minister. If you start this process early enough, there is no need for hurried decisions, later regretted.

The attitude between all parties is also extremely important.

David and I genuinely and deeply respect Jarrod's ministry and gifting. For a long time, we have sought both his and his older brother's spiritual advice. (We believe, honour the young and they will honour you.) We are astounded at his teaching and his willingness to step out for God, at his hunger for the Presence of God and the miraculous, and his desire to see revival in Hull, in our land and in the earth. In every way, we consider him a man of God.

That is not to say he doesn't have faults, - that's another issue. If we are to succeed in transition, we must not expect perfection. After all, we did OK and we aren't perfect either.

We also take every opportunity to support him, both with our actions and with our words and to let him know, we trust him and his decisions. We avoid at all costs:

"You're doing that wrong," "The people won't like that," "We've tried that and it didn't work," etc. and etc.

And yet because we are now his associate ministers, we take every chance to lighten his load, to say, "Can we do that for you?"

In the past, like many ministers of our generation, we have carried the load alone, and know how hard it can be. Today we are Aaron and Hur holding up his hands for as long as he wants and we are able. [Exodus 17:12] We have also noticed that this unity in leadership, this love and respect between the generations, has positively impacted the congregation and brought a wonderful balance of young fire and vision with older experience and wisdom.

The attitude of the older man is crucial. We do have experience and maturity on our side – let it show! For example with dedications, marriages and even funerals, we have let the congregation know; "You choose who you want, and you have our word that the other leader will not be offended, " – and we aren't. Any jealousy will destroy a successful transition. It must be said, though, I have noticed Jarrod is happy to dedicate the tiny, docile, newborn babies, but gives his father the wriggly, mischievous toddlers!

The attitude of the younger man is equally very important. He should deeply and sincerely respect the past, although perhaps imperfect. Appreciate the ground that has been ploughed, sown and watered, perhaps for many years, at deep personal sacrifice and sometimes with limited fruit. And acknowledge that any present success and growth is at least, in part, due to the older man's labour.

I respect Jarrod for the way he honours not only our past leadership but also the leaders before us down through the years. Appreciating the senior man's gifting, wisdom and experience is also important. Again Jarrod's attitude and appreciation of our gifting has certainly oiled the wheels of transition. He regularly and sincerely affirms our input, both in private and before the church. Only the other morning, he introduced David, who was the speaker, as "The father of the house". David stood up to preach to enthusiastic applause. Mutual respect, encouragement and affirmation are vital throughout the church family, but particularly between the generations and especially as any baton is handed over.

It is also important to acknowledge that relinquishing responsibility for your beloved church to a younger, less experienced man may come with mixed feelings and private, even sub-conscious heartache.

Around the time of transition, I had a troubling dream. I dreamt I was my present age, early sixties, and I was pregnant with triplets! I strongly, because of my age and their number, did not want these babies. I immediately dismissed abortion, knowing that although caring for these babies at my age would take what was left of my life, abortion, too, would potentially destroy me and my walk with God.

So in my dream, I decided I would have to carry the babies, give them birth, and then hand them over, or at least some of them, to leaders within the church. But then I decided I couldn't even do this because I would be deeply unhappy if the triplets weren't raised to my satisfaction. (I realise there could be control issues here!) I then decided there was no alternative but to sacrifice the rest of my life in rearing these babies, whom I knew I would love completely, but it was a burden I did not want to carry.

I woke up fearful and anxious, with no understanding of what the dream meant. Over breakfast, still upset, I shared with David, who immediately interpreted it as a deep, subconscious concern about handing over the care of the church I loved so much, to others less experienced.

It isn't always easy, but nothing worthwhile ever is. There comes a time in our lives when one of our main ministries is to prepare the next generation, to be their role models. To pass on our gifting, wisdom and experience and to encourage them, "Go for it, - stand on my shoulders, reach higher than I ever have and I will rejoice with you, knowing I have had a little part in it."

One of our Fathers and mentors in the faith was Eric Dando. When he died, on his funeral order of service it said, "Whatever you have learned or received or heard from me, or seen in me - put it into practice. And the God of peace will be with you." (Philippians 4:9) I hope he knows how many times in our ministry at a difficult place, we would say, "What would Pastor Dando have done?"

We have grown in these last years, from approximately 250 to 400 as a Fellowship, with around 70 different departments, praise God! And I remember in one of our recent conferences, standing in a packed auditorium of worshipping people, sensing the dynamic presence of God, with T.V. cameras around the hall, ready to distribute God's blessing even further and whispering, "Thank you God for allowing me to be a part of this."

I honour also our congregation, who while loving and embracing Jarrod and Vicky, and running without complaint with all the changes that have been made and are being made, have never faltered in their love, respect and appreciation of us and our ministry. Do not underestimate this, the people's attitude is very influential and can make or break any transition. Co-operation from the congregation, their love, respect, encouragement and impartiality, towards both parties, will ease changeover.

King David was not allowed to build the temple of the Lord but brought together all the materials to help his son Solomon build it and accomplish his own destiny. What better legacy can we give to the next generation than our release and blessing? And as we hand over the baton and they begin their run for the Kingdom, shout at the top of our voices, to the cheers of the congregation and heaven, and with all of God's authority behind us, "Go for it my son!"

Chapter 51
Leaving With Our Blessing (Our Natural Children)

"Mum, I'm leaving home", words that strike dread in the heart of every parent. Or at least that's certainly how I felt when each of my sons flew the nest.

Jason left home within weeks of us returning to the UK, and in fact, our son's futures were one of the reasons we had decided to return. Jason had been working very successfully in a Spanish Bank, but this was not what he wanted for his life. So within a short time of being in the UK, we drove to Cumbria, where Jason had secured a job, with a massive drop in salary, to work in an outdoor centre! He was twenty years old and didn't want his parents to ruin his credibility, so we stopped a mile down the road and watched as he walked away, rucksack on his back, to begin the life he had chosen.

This was very tough for us all. Jarrod missed his brother and best friend and David and I found it especially hard. But we had so many challenges at this time to distract us, including a new home and a new church to lead.

About two years later Jarrod, now about nineteen, announced his intention to go to Bible School in West Sussex. Although there was pride in this, I was also devastated. This was my last child and I felt too young to be childless.

On his last Sunday in Church, he sang his youth group an emotional song about friendship and I wept before the whole church as I told them God had told me He understood, as He had given His only Son. – Talk about "Drama!" Tissue boxes were being passed along the rows!

I blamed David because we had not had more children and his very reasonable answer was, "No matter how many children we had, one day they would all leave home," - but who wanted a reason! For some time I suffered quite severely from "empty nest syndrome." Who was I? What was now my role? Did my children still need me, - or even love me?

I had always been a full-time mother. In fact I admit, at that time, being slightly against mothers working. By the time the children were well settled in school and I might have pursued more of my own interests, David was in full-time ministry and I supported him and worked within the church, which could be scheduled around school hours. Even in their teens, I wanted to be there for them, because it's often at this age, that peer pressure causes our children to make bad decisions that potentially negatively affect their lives.

But now in the midst of this terrible emptiness, I began to see the value in maintaining a career and in having another life outside of being "Mum". Of course with childcare more available, young mothers today have a few more options. But I still say, wholeheartedly, that our children must come first and our time and attention are far more valuable to them than possessions, although I realise that many mothers work to provide essentials and not for extras.

Since that day my sons have provided for themselves; but because they have both led unusual lives, often with no guaranteed cheque at the end of the month, I have always let them know, in our home there would be a bed and a plate of food available for them. I wanted to give them a safety net, so they could feel free to launch out and be adventurous in God.

And just occasionally, they have taken us up on this offer. After a few years in outdoor education, Jason began to work in a Christian Aid

Agency. His salary had grown again in the last years, but now he took yet another decrease! I remember saying to him "Could just one of my sons get a job with a good salary to look after me and Dad in our old age?" But he reminded me, "Don't move the goalposts now Mum, you brought us up to believe money wasn't important and that God's will and personal fulfilment was!"

Especially during his time in Afghanistan and Kosovo, Jason would return home for that promised bed and a plate of food, to recuperate from the traumas he had faced.

Jarrod, too, after seven years in Bible school and related work, asked to return home to establish an itinerant ministry. It was supposed to be for a year but ended up being six. I did take board off Jarrod at this time. "Living by faith" is not the same as sponging off your parents and if this was God, we wanted Jarrod to prove Him financially. Being a good parent does not include being "God" to them.

Then again Jarrod and his wife called in this parental offer of bed and food during the Hull floods last summer. They were moving house and having relinquished their home, with all their belongings in the removal van, they were unable to reach the new house because of flooding. After several hours of detours, a tired voice came on the phone – "Mum, can we move in, we're wet through and homeless!"

Our children leave home, but we are still their parents. If we release them with our love and our blessing, they still come back, even if it's only for a short while. We talk regularly to both our sons and at times they ask our advice and opinion. We live vicariously through all the wonderful things they have accomplished and achieved. Their lives and travels have widened our horizons.

God lends us our children for a short time and He says to us, "Take this child and nurse it for me and I will reward you." (Exodus 2:9)

How great is that reward!

Chapter 52
Leaving With Our Blessing
(Our Spiritual Children)

"Mum, I'm leaving home", words that strike dread in the heart of every parent. Or at least that's certainly how I felt when each of my sons flew the nest. But although I dreaded life without them around on a daily basis, my heart was also filled with pride that my boys were now men, about to stand on their own two feet and be independent. My job was not only completed, but completed successfully.

Losing our natural children can bring mixed feelings, great pride and joy, but also tremendous pain. Almost as traumatic is when one of our spiritual children declares, "Pastor, I'm leaving." I don't believe I will ever hear this statement without being shocked and upset, and I have heard it many, many times.

But along with the pain of losing people we love, have taught and nurtured and may even now be sharing responsibility within the church, we should also be proud and grateful that they have reached such a place of maturity, God is leading them out into wider pastures.

Whenever this happens, David & I put aside our own feelings of loss and even disappointment, to say "God bless you, go with our blessing. And if this should only be for a season, or if for any reason this doesn't work out how you expected, please come home, the door is always open."

This isn't always easy to do, and it has often been at great personal and church cost, but it is important to do the right thing, simply because it is right.

I remember losing a young family some years ago, which had been very important within the fellowship, serving in several areas. On a personal level, we were also great friends. I regularly baby-sat their five beautiful children and they would often involve us socially in their home group activities. Many of us were extremely tearful on their last Sunday, and it was at least a couple of years before I could even think of them without feeling distressed at our loss.

In the church, the wife had been our worship leader and keyboard player and although we were a reasonable size, they left such a big hole in this ministry that David, once again, had to take up the guitar, something he hadn't done for years. The pain of loss was compounded by the fact that the church to which they moved, had several worship groups and many musicians! It was very hard to see, understand and accept God's hand in this.

I have to stress that this family moved honourably, giving us plenty of warning and in spite of our pain, we knew God was in this move, which was particularly to put the husband in a place of Christian influence in the secular media.

Not everyone leaves so honourably or so obviously in God's will. Another family has left us twice, the last time with only five days notice, abandoning ministries and responsibilities and leaving many hurting and bewildered people behind them. But even in those circumstances, we encouraged them to come to the fellowship to be prayed for, blessed and released.

Not all leaders react this way and we have often been upset at hearing that church or ministry leaders have resisted when people they have nurtured are moving on. In fact, in some cases, cursing them by declaring "You are not in God's will, you are rebellious, you will never fulfil your destiny - you are finished."

We leaders are not infallible. We need to admit; we don't always know God's will for each of our people. We also need to be open about our insecurities. We are not always as strong, resilient and capable as we appear. We, too, may feel hurt, rejected, worried about coping, disappointed that all we have sown will now bear fruit elsewhere, - and many other negative feelings.

But leaders, at these times, let's be mature, do the right thing and release our spiritual children with our blessing, and more than this, let them know "Come home anytime, we love you and are so proud of you." Let's be their safety net, so they can feel free to be adventurous in God. When we release them with our love and blessing, it's so much easier for them to come home or simply to seek our advice.

And if you are the one leaving, go honourably; give your pastor time to fill ministry gaps. And please don't forget to thank your leaders for all their teaching, time and discipline, for covering your mistakes and for trusting you enough to allow you to serve with them.

There is a principle, in the Bible, that what we sow, we reap. (Galatians 6:7) When we sow love, respect and honour, this is also what we receive. When we leave one church or ministry in a godly, honourable way, we are building a good foundation for our next ministry to succeed. But if we sow dishonour and disrespect, this too will bring negative fruit, potentially spoiling future ministry.

And leaders, - when we release with blessing, even though our heart is breaking, God will fill those gaps that have been left, not only in the Fellowship, but in our hearts.

David & I have spiritual children serving God all over the world. Each one in going has broken our hearts, but each one has also filled us with great joy, that we have had just a tiny part in their maturing.

God lends us even our spiritual children, sometimes for such a short time and He says to us, "Take this child and nurse it for me and I will reward you." (Exodus 2:9)

How great is that reward!

EPILOGUE

When I began to collect together these articles ready to put into book form, I fully expected that many of them would feel dated. They were written at least a decade ago for the Assemblies of God monthly magazine "Joy". But I found that they were mostly still relevant, that our world has not changed so much. We are still in the midst of financial insecurity, the moral decline in our nation and indeed the western world continues. We continue to struggle with the sensitive and painful issue of immigration on our small island. And to be a Christian today is similar to walking a tightrope, as the Bible and the attitudes and indeed the laws of our nation, oppose each other.

It would be so easy to despair and to ask ourselves, "Will things ever change?"

I was in this place when Jarrod handed us his latest book, "500: Are we at the dawn of a new era of glory?" I read this book on the long return journey from Scotland to East Yorkshire where we live. The miles passed with me simultaneously sobbing and worshipping! This book brings together the prophetic words of proven men and women of God down the years, who are saying the same thing, "Now is the time, God is about to move!" Some even indicating that this would include the transforming of our traditional churches, something very close to my heart! All I could cry out was, "God do it, turn our nation around, but please let me see it, do it in my lifetime!"

I have for many years lived my life by this maxim, - If we do what we can do, God will do what we cannot do. Yes - we must live as salt and light in our world, we must live in this nation or wherever God has placed us, as His Ambassadors and representatives of His Kingdom. And our God is so amazing, as even in this, God strengthens us! One of my most treasured scriptures is 2 Peter 1:3 "His divine power has given us everything we need for life and godliness through our knowledge of Him who called us by His own glory and goodness." Yet deep in my heart I know it is not enough, what our world needs is a fresh, mighty, glorious and transforming outpouring of God's Holy Spirit.

ABOUT THE AUTHOR

Marion Cooper (along with her husband David) have been in ministry since the 1970's, firstly in church eldership in Newport, South Wales, followed by 10 years as missionaries leading a church in Gibraltar.

On return to the UK in 1988 they became senior leaders of Revive Church (called "New Life Church" at the time) and led the church until 2005.

Now officially retired they continue to speak, travel, support leaders and write, but also have lots of fun with their grandson, Zachary.

They have two grown sons, Jason and Jarrod.

Printed in Great Britain
by Amazon